HISTORIC
German Newspapers
ONLINE

Compiled by
Ernest Thode

Genealogical Publishing Company
Baltimore, Maryland

Published by Genealogical Publishing Company
Baltimore, Maryland, 2014

Library of Congress Catalog Card Number 2014952975

ISBN 978-0-8063-2005-2

Made in the United States of America

Contents

Introduction

Historic German-language newspapers are at least as useful as their English-language American counterparts for genealogical research. Unfortunately, for reasons of language, accessibility, and typeface, they have not been heavily used. However, I contend that any search for a German or Eastern European ancestor is incomplete without looking in German-language newspapers for that area. You have not done your due diligence unless you have performed a thorough search of all the resources available. There are now thousands of titles online, many scanned with OCR software, some full-text searchable, and others viewable by going chronologically and page by page (like the olden days of cranking a microfilm reader).

For American German-language newspapers, the standard bibliography is Karl J. R. Arndt and May Olson's *The German Language Press of the Americas*, which gives locations of holdings and years held, as well as details about editors, publishers, political viewpoint, and circulation figures. For research in European newspapers, there are paper, microfilm, and microfiche copies at the German Newspaper Museum in Dortmund, the International Newspaper Museum in Aachen, and the German Press Research Institute in Bremen. Dortmund is the research center for scholars who need whole runs of a newspaper; they can come in person or use Interlibrary Loan. Aachen holds rare first editions, final editions, and historic editions (world events, famous dates) from all over the world, and will scan them and make CD copies. The University of Bremen specializes in study of some of the earliest German newspapers and special topics such as propaganda papers.

I have arbitrarily set my definition of "historic" newspapers at 50 years or older. However, in the case of a continuing run online I include more current editions. I also include a few annual school reports and wartime casualty lists because of their genealogical relevance. Few historic German newspapers have been digitized until the past few years, though most current German newspapers have published electronic editions for more than a decade. As I began collecting information, I was astounded to learn how many German papers are digitally online. They are truly worldwide, from Tanunda, Australia; Morogoro, Tanzania; Zhelezhnodororozhny, Russia; Tsientsin, China; and El Reno, Oklahoma, USA. Mostly they are freely accessible, put online by national libraries, universities, and museums, even international consortia such as Europeana. Some sites have more than 100 titles, such as Compact Memory and ANNO, with titles from the entire Austro-Hungarian Empire. I have found 2,000 digitized titles online at numerous public, private, and commercial sites. I will describe some of the most significant ones.

ANNO is hosted by the Austrian National Library at http://anno.onb.ac.at. It has digitized millions of pages in hundreds of titles from the entire Austro-Hungarian Empire, including especially capitals of provinces. The years 1700–1875 for the Austro-Hungarian Empire are 97% digitized and full-text searchable within a given issue. World War I era papers from 1914 to 1918 are also searchable. The site is user-friendly and has an English interface available. If you are interested in the Zagreb, Croatia, click on *Agramer Zeitung,* because you learned in this book that Agram is the former German name for Zagreb. When you click on the title, a list of years appears (1841–1912). The years in bold blue type are online. Click on a year to find the dates available. Then click on a date in bold blue. Click on the thumbnail view of the page you want to look at. One way to get acquainted with a paper is to look at the ads first, then regular-appearing sections Here the thumbnails help. On April 26, 1858, on page 4, you can see an advertisement for passenger steamers *(Passagier-Dampfboote)*, some governmental edicts *(Edikt)*, an executor's notice *(Aufforderung)* for the estate of Martin Medle, a railroad stock sale *(Subskriptions-Eröffnung)*, a request for a home health helper (*Zur Pflege einer Kranken*), a pharmacist's assistant *(Apotheker-Gehilfe)* wanted, a sale *(Lizitation)* of furniture and cows, and a room for rent *(Wohnung zu vermiethen)*. 97% of ANNO papers up to 1875 are full-text searchable, subject to the limitations of OCR technology.

Bavarica is hosted by the Munich Digitization Center of the Bavarian State Library. For English, click the British flag in the upper right-hand corner. Coverage includes Bavaria, with the Palatinate, plus a few other areas, such as Hessen, that were once Bavarian or had close interactions with Bavaria. It has some unique useful features. The entire data set is full-text searchable, and certain common names and locations are automatically recognized by the OCR software; if the character reader first "sees" Wiiheln, the software automatically improves it to Wilhelm; if it first "sees" Heldclbcrg, it automatically improves it to Heidelberg. Suppose you know that your ancestor Sophia Fickeisen came from somewhere in Bavaria. That means the Bavarica site is a logical place to look for her. If you type in "sophia fickeisen" you will note that one result shows a score of 100%, which obviously indicates a good match. Click on that match and the name Sophia Fickeisen is highlighted on the page. If the text seems too small, click on the +0.05 increment a few times to zoom in. (You may need several clicks.) Whether or not you can read German *Fraktur* fonts, you can see that something happened to Sophia on 21 September 1854 and should also be able to make out Nordamerika, which is a clue that this has to do with her emigration. And it turns out that she was from Cusel (now spelled Kusel), which was in the Bavarian Palatinate (Pfalz). The Pfalz is not a part of present-day Bavaria, but it was from 1815 to 1945. The newspaper is an official one, a *Beilage* (supplement) to the *Königlich-bayerisches Kreis-Amtsblatt der Pfalz* (Royal Bavarian County Official Newspaper of the Palatinate), page 350. There is more about her family there as well. Official government papers are among the best European genealogical sources.

BNF is the *Bibliotheque Nationale de France*, www.bnf.fr, the French National Library in Strasbourg. Its German-language papers include battlefront papers from World War I and some official publications from Alsace and Lorraine—Colmar, Haguenau, Mulhouse, and Strasbourg.

Compact Memory, compactmemory.de, has more than 100 German-language Jewish newspapers. There are 8 full-text papers online, including some of the most important long-run papers available.

Google Books, **books.google.de**, is far and away the most extensive digitizer of historic German newspapers, especially the official government gazettes held in Google's partner libraries and institutions. Even though it may seem odd to include newspapers in the category of books, it may help to remember that newspapers can be bound in hard covers, and they are found as bound volumes in libraries. Incidentally, German newspapers from Pittsburgh and New Orleans are still on the Google News site, (separate from Google Books), but Google stopped adding papers to Google News in 2011. It is important to remember to use the German version of the site, http://books.google.de, and it wouldn't hurt to add German as a language in your browser's settings. Google results actually differ based on the country and language of the search. Look for titles that have common newspaper titles and where available pick thumbnails that look like newspaper pages. Some of the most frequent German titles of government papers include *Allgemeine Zeitung, Amtsblatt, Anzeiger, Bote or Bothe, Intelligenzblatt, Regierungsblatt, Tagblatt, Tageblatt, Tagesblatt, Tagsblatt, Wochenblatt,* and *Zeitung. Blatt* may also be set off with a hyphen and capitalized.

As an example, suppose you are looking for your ancestor Berthold Hitscherich. Look in the German Google Books. He lived in Rastatt and was paid restitution (for fire or wind damage?) according to the 1868 *Großherzoglich Badisches Regierungsblatt.* If you try to replicate this and do not get a match, make sure you looked in the German version, books.google.de, and that you spelled the name right.

Or let's say you are looking for Kreszenz Hublochner. You will find her name listed in the *Bayerisches Central-Polizei-Blatt,* the police gazette. In it you will find her in an index referring to #9182, where you learn her birthdate, 16 Jun (18)44, her birthplace Rudelzhausen in the parish of Enzelhausen, her maiden name Hirmer, that she is widowed, and that she was living in Berg in the district of Landshut in 1900.

It's not just people to look for. If you know a (small) place where your ancestor (or several of your ancestor's associates) came from, say Burtreit, you can possibly find information about the community (Hoheneggelkose) and the county (Landshut), possibly the number of houses or the population, possibly some of the occupations and industries, possibly some of the surnames, maybe who was called (or failed to show up) for military service—it's hard telling. Even if learning about the community is not your main goal, it is still useful background information.

The **Deutsches Historisches Museum (DHM)** (German Historical Museum) in Berlin hosts several newspapers from historic periods—World War I, World War II, the Nazi period. Their *Objektdatenbank* (database of objects) at www.dhm.de/datenbank/dhm has more than 550,000 items online, including newspaper pages.

DiFMOE stands for *Digitales Forum Mittel- und Osteuropa,* the Digital Forum for Central and Eastern Europe, at **www.difmoe.eu/?content=Periodika.** You need to choose *Zeitungen/Zeitschriften.* Most newspapers are full-text searchable. German ones extend as far from Germany as Riga, Latvia; Hermannstadt, Romania (Transylvania); and Lodz, Poland.

DigiPress is an ongoing retro-digitizing program for Bavarian newspapers by the Bavarian State Library in Munich, http://digipress.digitale-sammlungen.de/. There were 49 regional Bavarian newspapers in it as of July 2014. Click on the newspaper name; the years available are in bold; click on the year, then the date in bold.

Europeana is a website, www.europeana.eu, hosted by a major consortium of national libraries highlighting digitized European cultural items in general, including newspapers. Funding for the project runs from 2012 to 2015, though the site will of course remain online. German-language newspapers from Austria, Belgium, Estonia, Germany, Latvia, Poland, and Ukraine are included. An English interface is available. All types of matches may be included in search results—photos, ephemera, maps, as well as newspapers. I suggest that you first get a search result for your place or person of interest, then refine it on the left-hand side by media type, language, year, and providing country. Or find a newspaper that might cover your location of interest and just go through it page by page.

The **Friedrich Ebert Stiftung**, fes.de, (the Friedrich Ebert Foundation) is devoted to the history of the labor movement, socialism, and the Social Democratic Party in Germany. From www.library.fes.de go to *Digitale Bibliothek* then *Zeitschriften Digitalisierungen*. The most useful genealogically are the occupational publications for saddlers, railroadmen, gardeners, bookbinders, tailors, etc. Images are JPEGs.

HathiTrust is a consortium of 135 major US university libraries that puts holdings online at www.hathitrust.org. In 2014 there are about 4 billion pages of material online. A few of the participating libraries providing German titles are Cornell University, Harvard University, the New York Public Library, Princeton University, and the Universities of California, Michigan, and Wisconsin. You can first search the catalog (I would suggest by region), then go to a pertinent title. There is some overlap with Google Books and Open Library. Books or pages can be downloaded as PDFs.

The **Tessmann Library** in Bozen (Italian name Bolzano, Italy) is a legacy from Dr. Friedrich Tessmann, who collected material on the South Tirol and other Alpine territories, so there are materials from Italy, Austria, and Switzerland. Besides being a regular library and scientific library, the newspaper library http://dza.tessmann.it/tessmannPortal/ has been online since 2012, with an English-language interface available by clicking on the word "english" at the top of the right column. There are 30 German-language newspapers represented from 1796 to 1974.

Some of the following universities are actually called *Hochschule* or *Technische Universität* and may also be affiliated with a state library.

The **University of Bonn** has placed 100 titles from the Rhine and Sieg valleys online at digitale-sammlungen.ulb.uni-bonn.de/.

The **University of Bremen** specializes in older German-language newspapers. Their digitized newspapers are all from the 1600s.

The **Technical University of Darmstadt,** http://tudigit.ulb.tu-darmstadt.de/, has 20 titles from former Hessen-Darmstadt and Rheinhessen, including Bingen, Darmstadt, Offenbach, Mainz, Worms, and other places.

The **University of Dresden** at http://digital.slub-dresden.de/ has several clockmakers' publications online.

The **University of Düsseldorf** at http://digital.ub.uni-duesseldorf.de/ covers the old Duchies of Jülich and Berg and the Prussian District of Düsseldorf, 12 titles. There is a complete run of Düsseldorf governmental gazettes from 1816 to 1987.

The **University of Frankfurt am Main** has 23 titles at sammlungen.ub.uni-frankfurt.de/periodika/, nearly all covering the World War I era. The university also provided many of the periodicals digitized at Compact Memory.

The **University of Fulda** at http://fuldig.hs-fulda.de places publications from Fulda online.The **University of Heidelberg,** http://zeitungen-digital.uni-hd.de/, has 98 titles, including World War I newspapers and newspapers from all locations about the 500th anniversary of the university in 1886.

The **University of Jena** has 61 newspapers from Thuringia, plus specialized church and school newspapers at zs.thulb.uni-jena.de. One of the papers is the *Allgemeine Auswanderungs-Zeitung*, the major emigration paper published in Rudolstadt.

The **University of Münster**, http://sammlungen.ulb.uni-muenster.de, has newspapers from Münster and Bochum, as well as a few theatrical papers.

ZEFYS is hosted by the State Library in Berlin, in association with the Institute for Prussian Cultural Heritage. An English version is at http://zefys.staatsbibliothek-berlin. de/en/. It is the newspaper information source for Prussian publications, especially official gazettes, the press of the DDR (former East Germany), and some others published abroad in the German language. There were 141,000 issues of 137 historic papers on ZEFYS in September 2014. You can do a full-text site search or click on the newspaper, then the year, then the date.

At the time of publication the most active projects seem to be at ANNO, Europeana, Google Books Germany, the University of Jena, and ZEFYS. For whatever region, southern German sites have more active than their northern counterparts. The USA lags behind, but don't forget that microfilm and hard copies exist at numerous libraries, archives, and historical societies (see Arndt & Olson's *The German-Language Press of the Americas*). Perhaps some of our wealthy readers or German-American foundations will fund digitization projects.

The types of genealogical information you can sometimes find include baptisms and weddings from churches, especially in capital city papers; births, marriages, and deaths from civil registrations, especially in capital city papers; intentions to emigrate, especially in governmental papers; auctions, governmental papers; wanted criminals, police gazettes; general advertisements; trade news in trade journals; lists of church donors in church and governmental papers; lists of compensation paid to fire and storm victims in governmental papers; lists of hotel guests in big city and spa papers; lists of pupils (and their parents) in annual school reports; lists of spa visitors (in papers in spa cities); appointments to office, transfers, promotions, retirements, and deaths. There are also unexpected finds pertaining to the USA, such as a list of Waldeck soldiers in North America in the American Revolution found in a Waldeck government paper; the engagement in Newark, New Jersey, of a couple from Kesmark, Slovakia; and a description of emigrants headed for Cincinnati in an emigration paper. These are gems you cannot afford to miss. You need to look for the regional paper for your ancestor's German county seat, the government paper (Bavaria, Baden, Hessen, a Prussian province, etc.), and the daily paper of the closest large city for your ancestor.

To use this book, first look for your place of interest in the Places section to see what papers are online for your area of interest. In the next section, Titles (note that titles beginning with *Der*, *Die*, or *Das* are found in the D's; use the same form as in the Places section), see a general description of the coverage and a short abbreviation for the URL (the website). Finally, you can find the URL of your desired website. For papers found in Polish archives, you may need to try under www.polona.pl/dlibra, which includes the various regional archives.

Ernest Thode

Key	Site	URL
Aargau	Canton Aargau Library	www.ag.ch/kantonsbibliothek
AAS	Austrian Academy of Science	www.oeaw.ac.at
Abendblatt	Hamburger Abendblatt	http://suche.abendblatt.de/ashao/calendar.php
A-Bib	Anarchistische Bibliothek	www.a-bibliothek.org
ABLIT	Abenteuerliteratur	www.abenteuer-literatur.de
ALO	Austrian Literature Online	www.literature.at
Altenburg	Kreisarchiv Altenburg	www.altenburg.eu
Amberg	Staatsarchiv Amberg	www.gda.bayern.de/archive/amberg/
Ancestry	Ancestry.com	www.ancestry.com
ANL	Austrian National Library	www.onb.ac.at/en/
ANNO	AustriaN Newspapers Online	http://anno.onb.ac.at
ArbZ	Arbeiter-Zeitung	www.arbeiter-zeitung.at
Archivaria	Archivaria	www.archivaria.com
ArchOrg	Archive.org	www.archive.org
Baden	Badische Landesbibliothek	www.blb-karlsruhe.de
Baeck	Leo Baeck Institute	www.lbi.org
Bavarica	Bavarica	http://bavarica.digitale-sammlungen.de
BBC	Baltycka Biblioteka Cyfrowa	http://bibliotekacyfrowa.eu
Belg Arch	National Archives of Belgium	http://arch.arch.be

Key	Site	URL
Belg Lib	Royal Library of Belgium	www.kbr.be
Berlin Lib	Berlin State Library	http://staatsbibliothek-berlin.de/en/
BF	Burgenländische Freiheit	http://bf-archiv.at
Bio	Biodiversity Library	www.biodiversitylibrary.org
Blank	Albrecht Blank	www.albrecht-blank.eu
Breslau	Wroclaw University Library (Breslau)	www.bibliotekacyfrowa.pl/dlibra/
BritLib	British Library	www.bl.uk
BSL	Bayerische Landesbibliothek	http://www.bayerische-landesbibliothek-online.de
CH	Swiss Confederation	www.admin.ch
Chron	Chronicling America	http://chroniclingamerica.loc.gov/newspapers/
Cieszyn	Cieszyn Library	http://biblioteka.cieszyn.pl
Colo	Colorado Historic Newspapers	www.coloradohistoricnewspapers.org
CompMem	Compact Memory (Jewish)	http://compactmemory.de
CRL	Center for Research Libraries	www.crl.edu
Croatia	Croatian Historic Newspapers	http://dnc.nsk.hr/newspapers/English.aspx
Dach	Dachau Municipal Archive	http://archiv.dachau.de
DiFMOE	Digitales Forum Mittel- und Osteuropa	www.difmoe.eu
DigiBern	DigiBern	http://digibern.ch/en/index.html
DigiPress	DigiPress	http://digipress.digitale-sammlungen.de

Key	Site	URL
Dilibri	Digital Library Rheinland-Pfalz	www.dilibri.de
Dithm	Dithmarschen Wiki	www.dithmarschen-wiki.de
DLS	Digital Library of Slovenia	www.dlib.sl
DSL	Saxon State Library Dresden	www.slub-dresden.de
Elbing	Elbing Library	http://dlibra.bibliotekaelblaska.pl/dlibra/
E-Lib	Swiss Electronic Library	www.e-lib.ch/en/
Estonia	National Archives of Estonia	http://rahvusarhiiv.ra.ee/en/
Eur	Europeana	www.europeana.eu/
Eutin	Eutin State Library	www.lb-eutin.de/
FES	Friedrich Ebert Foundation	www.fes.de
France	French National Library	www.bnf.fr/en/tools/a.welcome_to_the_bnf.html
Gale	Cengage	www.gale.cengage.com
GateBay	Gateway Bayern (Bavaria)	www.gateway-bayern.de
GHM	German Historical Museum	www.dhm.de
GNL	German National Library	www.dnb.de/EN/Kataloge/kataloge_node.html
Goo	Google Books	http://books.google.de
Goo News	Google Historic Newspaper Archive	http://news.google.com/newspapers
Gpulse	Germanpulse	www.germanpulse.com
Hathi	HathiTrust	www.hathitrust.org

Key	Site	URL
Hennef	Hennef City Library	http://da.stadt-hennef.de
Hlgnst	Heiligenstadt City Archive	http://heilbad-heiligenstadt.de/stadtinformation/stadtarchiv.html
Humb	Humboldt University Berlin	www.hu-berlin.de/suche/
Hungary	Electronic Periodical Archive Hungary	http://epa.Oszk.hu
IHS	Indiana Historical Society	www.indianahistory.org
Jag	Jagellionian Digital Library	http://jbc.bj.uj.edu.pl/dlibra/
Jud Allg	Juedische Allgemeine Zeitung	www.juedische-allgemeine.de
KDL	Kentucky Digital Library	http://kdl.kyvl.org
Kosz	Koszalin State Archive	www.koszalin.ap.gov.pl
Kram	Kramerius	http://kramerius.nkp.cz
Kuja	Kujawsko-Pomorska Digital Library	http://kpbc.umk.pl/dlibra/
Latvia	Latvian National Library	www.lnb.lv/en
Leipzig	Leipzig City Museum	www.stadtgeschichtliches-museum-leipzig.de/index_en.php
Liecht	Eliechtensteinensia	www.eliechtensteinensia.li
Lippe	Lippe Library Detmold	www.lib-detmold.de
Lpzg	Leipzig City Museum	www.stadtgeschichtliches-museum-leipzig.de/index_en.php
Lux	Luxemburgensia	www.luxemburgensia.bnl.lu
Meck	Mecklenburg-Vorpommern State Library	http://wafr.lbmv.de/search.php
MICHAEL	Multilingual Inventory Cultural Heritage	www.michael-culture.eu/

Key	Site	URL
NAUSA	North American Emigration Center	http://www.nausa.uni-oldenburg.de/pionier/frame.html
Newsbank	Newsbank	www.newsbank.com
Newspapers	America's Historic Newspapers	www.newsbank.com
NRWLib	North Rhine-Westphalia Library	www.hbz-nrw.de/recherche/
NZZ	Neue Zürcher Zeitung	www.nzz.ch
OKHist	Oklahoma History	www.okhistory.org/research/newspapers
OPACP	OPAC Plus	https://openlibrary.org
Poland	Polish National Library	www.bn.org.pl/en/digital-resources/polona/
Poznan	Greater Poland Digital Library	www.wbc.poznan.pl/dlibra/
Raether	Raether Buch	www.raether-buch.de/
Rendsbg	Rendsburg Municipal Archive	www.rendsburg.de/tourismus-freizeit-kultur/museen-archive.html
RERO	REseau ROmand (western Switzerland)	http://newspaper.archives.rero.ch
RheinM	Rhine-Main Library in Wiesbaden	www.hs-rm.de/bibliothek
Sandusky	Sandusky Public Library (Ohio)	http://sanduskyhistory.blogspot.com/2007/11/
SBgZ	Siebenbürgische Zeitung	www.siebenbuerger.de/zeitung/
Schaffh	Schaffhauser Nachrichten	www.shn.ch
Silesia	Silesian Digital Library	www.sbc.org.pl/dlibra
Simplic	Simplicissimus	www.simplicissimus.info
Spiegel	Der Spiegel	www.spiegel.de

Key	Site	URL
SPO	Scripta Paedagogica Online	http://bbf.dipf.de/scripta-paedagogica-online
Swarth	Swarthmore College Library	www.swarthmore.edu
Sweden	Royal Library of Sweden	www.kb.se/english/
Switz	Swiss National Library	www.nb.admin.ch
TCO	Texas Cultures Online	texashistory.unt.edu/explore/collections/TCO/
Tessmann	Tessmann Library	www.tessmann.it
Trove	Trove (Australia)	https://trove.nla.gov.au/newspaper
TX	Portal to Texas History	http://texashistory.unt.edu/explore/collections/TDNP/
UAUGS	University and State Library of Augsburg	www.bibliothek.uni-augsburg.de/
UBERN	University of Bern (Switzerland)	www.ub.unibe.ch
UBIEL	University of Bielefeld	http://ds.ub.uni-bielefeld.de/viewer/
UBONN	University of Bonn	http://s2w.hbz-nrw.de/ulbbn
UBREM	University of Bremen	http://brema.suub.uni-bremen.de
UBRUN	Technical University of Braunschweig	www.biblio.tu-bs.de/benutzung/flyer/digibib-bs2.pdf
UCLAU	Technical University of Clausthal	http://www.ub.tu-clausthal.de/en/literatur-suchen/ezb/
UCOTT	Technical University of Cottbus www.b-tu.de/b-tu/	
UDARM	Technical University of Darmstadt	www.tu-darmstadt.de/index.en.jsp
UDRES	State and University Library of Dresden	www.slub-dresden.de/en/home/
UDUS	University of Düsseldorf	http://digital.ub.uni-duesseldorf.de/

Key	Site	URL
UFBRG	University of Freiburg (Baden)	www.ub.uni-freiburg.de/?id=fz
UFFM	University of Frankfurt am Main	http://sammlungen.ub.uni-frankfurt.de/
UFRIB	University of Fribourg (Switzerland)	http://www.unifr.ch/intman/
UFULD	Fulda Technical Institute	http://fuldig.hs-fulda.de/viewer/
UGDA	Gdańsk Polytechnic Institute	www.pg.edu.pl
UGOT	University of Göttingen	http://gdz.sub.uni-goettingen.de/gdz/
UGREI	University of Greifswald	http://digibib.ub.uni-greifswald.de/
UHAL	University of Halle-Wittenberg	http://bibliothek.uni-halle.de/dbib/digital/
UHBG	University of Hamburg	www.sub.uni-hamburg.de/home.html
UHEID	University of Heidelberg	www.ub.uni-heidelberg.de/helios/
UJENA	Technical University of Jena (Thuringia)	www.thulb.uni-jena.de/thulb2/Recherche/
UKASL	University of Kassel (Hesse)	www.uni-kassel.de/ub/index.php
UKIEL	University of Kiel	http://dibiki.ub.uni-kiel.de/viewer/
UKLN	University of Cologne (Köln)	www.ub.uni-koeln.de/digital/digitsam/index_ger.html
UMST	University of Münster	www.ulb.uni-muenster.de/recherche/digibib/
UMUN	University of Munich (München)	www.ub.uni-muenchen.de/en/electronic-media/
UOLD	University of Oldenburg	www.bis.uni-oldenburg.de/ueber-uns/organisation/digitale-bibliothek/
UpAust	Upper Austria State Library	www.landesbibliothek.at/
UPULA	University of Pola (Pula) (Croatia)	http://ino.com.hr/polaer_tagblatt.html

Key	Site	URL
UREG	University of Regensburg	http://rzblx1.uni-regensburg.de/ezeit/
UROS	University of Rostock	www.ub.uni-rostock.de/ub/xdlib/dlib_xde.shtml
USTR	University of Strasbourg (France)	www.bnu.fr/en/collections/digital-library
UTARTU	University of Tartu (Estonia)	http://www.utlib.ee/
UTUEB	University of Tübingen	https://tue.ibs-bw.de/
WikiComm	Wikimedia Commons	http://commons.wikimedia.org/wiki/Main_Page
WikiS	WikiSource	http://de.wikisource.org
ZEFYS	ZEFYS Zeitungsinformationssystem	http://zefys.staatsbibliothek-berlin.de/en/
Zeit	Die Zeit	www.zeit.de
ZVDD	Central List of Digitized Publications	www.zvdd.de/startseite/

Country	Published at	Title	Notes
Argentina	Buenos Aires	Argentinisches Wochenblatt	
Australia	Adelaide	Adelaider Deutsche Zeitung	South Australia
Australia	Adelaide	Südaustralische Zeitung	South Australia
Australia	Tanunda and Adelaide	Süd Australische Zeitung	South Australia
Austria	Baden	Badener Bezirks-Blatt	Lower Austria
Austria	Baden	Badener Zeitungen	Lower Austria
Austria	Bludenz	Anzeiger für die Bezirke Bludenz und Montafon	Vorarlberg
Austria	Braunau am Inn	Neue Warte am Inn	Upper Austria
Austria	Bregenz	Bregenzer Wochenblatt	Vorarlberg
Austria	Bregenz	Bregenzer/Vorarlberger Tagblatt	Vorarlberg
Austria	Bregenz	Der Vorarlberger	Vorarlberg
Austria	Bregenz	Vorarlberger Landes-Zeitung	Vorarlberg
Austria	Bregenz	Vorarlberger Volksblatt	Vorarlberg
Austria	Dornbirn	Der Vorarlberger Volksfreund	Vorarlberg
Austria	Dornbirn	Vorarlberger Wacht	Vorarlberg
Austria	Feldkirch	Feldkircher Anzeiger	Vorarlberg
Austria	Feldkirch	Feldkircher Wochenblatt	Vorarlberg
Austria	Grätz	Grätzer Zeitung	Styria
Austria	Graz	Akademische Frauenblätter	academic women's paper

Country	Published at	Title	Notes
Austria	Graz	Allgemeine Eisenbahn-Zeitung	railroad paper
Austria	Graz	Arbeiterwille	labor paper
Austria	Graz	Frauenblätter	women's paper
Austria	Graz	Grazer Mittags-Zeitung	Styria
Austria	Graz	Grazer Tagblatt	Styria
Austria	Graz	Grazer Volksblatt	Styria
Austria	Graz	Grazer Zeitung	Styria
Austria	Graz	Steyermärkische Intelligenz-Blätter der Grätzer Zeitung	Styria
Austria	Hainburg an der Donau	Niederösterreichischer Grenzbote	Lower Austria
Austria	Innsbruck	Andreas Hofer Wochenblatt	Alpine paper
Austria	Innsbruck	Der Alpenfreund	Alpine paper
Austria	Innsbruck	Der Bote für Tirol	Tirol
Austria	Innsbruck	Innsbrucker Nachrichten	Tirol
Austria	Innsbruck	Innsbrucker Zeitung	Tirol
Austria	Innsbruck	Innzeitung	Tirol
Austria	Innsbruck	Kaiserlich-Königlich privilegirter Bothe von und für Tirol und Vorarlberg	Tirol & Vorarlberg
Austria	Innsbruck	Südtiroler Heimat	South Tirol
Austria	Innsbruck	Südtiroler Ruf	regional paper
Austria	Innsbruck	Tiroler Zeitung	Catholic

Country	Published at	Title	Notes
Austria	Innsbruck	Ynnsbruckische Mittwochige Ordinari-Zeitung	Tirol
Austria	Ischl/Bad Ischl	Ischler Bade-Liste	spa visitors
Austria	Klagenfurt	Carinthia	Carinthia
Austria	Klagenfurt	Klagenfurter Zeitung	Carinthia
Austria	Klosterneuburg	Jahresbericht des N. ö. Landes-Realgymnasiums in Klosterneuburg	annual school report
Austria	Krems an der Donau	Jahresbericht über die nied. Österr. Landes-Oberrealschule in Krems	annual school report
Austria	Krems an der Donau	Österreichische Land-Zeitung	agricultural
Austria	Lienz	Lienzer Zeitung	Tirol
Austria	Linz	Amtliche Linzer Zeitung	Upper Austria
Austria	Linz	Linzer Tagespost	Upper Austria
Austria	Linz	Linzer Volksblatt	Upper Austria
Austria	Linz	Linzer Zeitung	Upper Austria
Austria	Linz	Oesterreichisches Bürgerblatt	Upper Austria
Austria	Linz	Unsere Zeitung	Austrian veterans paper
Austria	Linz; Krumau	Böhmerwald-Volksbote	political paper
Austria	Neulengbach	Neulengbacher Zeitung (Wienerwald-Bote)	Lower Austria
Austria	Pottenstein	Triestingtaler und Priestingtaler Wochenblatt	Lower Austria
Austria	Ried	Innviertler Heimatblatt	Upper Austria

Country	Published at	Title	Notes
Austria	Salzburg	Amts- und Intelligenz-Blatt von Salzburg	Salzburg
Austria	Salzburg	Königlich baierisches Intelligenzblatt des Salzach-Kreises	Bavaria at that time
Austria	Salzburg	Königlich baierisches Salzach-Blatt-Kreis	Bavaria at that time
Austria	Salzburg	Landes-Regierungsblatt für das Herzogthum Salz burg	Salzburg
Austria	Salzburg	Medicinisch-chirurgische Zeitung	surgical paper
Austria	Salzburg	Oberdeutsche Staatszeitung	Salzburg
Austria	Salzburg	Polizei-Blatt für das Herzogthum Salzburg	Salzburg
Austria	Salzburg	Salzburger Chronik	Salzburg
Austria	Salzburg	Salzburger Intelligenzblatt	Salzburg
Austria	Salzburg	Salzburger Volksblatt	Salzburg
Austria	Salzburg	Salzburger Wacht	Salzburg
Austria	Schwechat	Die Volkspost	Lower Austria
Austria	St. Pölten	Eggenburger Zeitung	Lower Austria
Austria	St. Pölten	Sankt Pöltener Diözesanblatt	Catholic diocesan paper
Austria	Steyr	Die Judenfrage	500 years U Heidelberg
Austria	Tulln	Brand Aus	Lower Austria firemen's paper
Austria	Wien/Vienna	12 Uhr Blatt	daily
Austria	Wien/Vienna	Allgemeine Automobil-Zeitung	automobile paper
Austria	Wien/Vienna	Allgemeine Bau-Zeitung	construction paper

Country	Published at	Title	Notes
Austria	Wien/Vienna	Allgemeine Land- und forstwirthschaftliche Zeitung	agricultural and forest paper
Austria	Wien/Vienna	Allgemeine Literatur-Zeitung zunächst für das katholische Deutschland	literature paper
Austria	Wien/Vienna	Allgemeine musikalische Zeitung	music paper
Austria	Wien/Vienna	Allgemeine Österreichische Gerichts-Zeitung	judicial newspaper
Austria	Wien/Vienna	Allgemeine Sport-Zeitung	sports paper
Austria	Wien/Vienna	Allgemeines Reichs-Gesetz- und Regierungsblatt für das Kaiserthum Oesterreich	laws for Austrian Empire
Austria	Wien/Vienna	An der schönen blauen Donau	music paper
Austria	Wien/Vienna	Arbeiter Schachzeitung	chess paper
Austria	Wien/Vienna	Arbeiterinnen-Zeitung	women's political paper
Austria	Wien/Vienna	Arbeiter-Zeitung	Austrian labor paper
Austria	Wien/Vienna	Arbeiter-Zeitung	political paper
Austria	Wien/Vienna	Armeeblatt	Austrian army paper
Austria	Wien/Vienna	Austria: Tagblatt für Handel und Gewerbe	business and industry paper
Austria	Wien/Vienna	Auszug aus der Tagespresse	WWI press reports
Austria	Wien/Vienna	Bade- und Reise-Journal	travel guide
Austria	Wien/Vienna	Beilage zur politischen Chronik	parliamentary news
Austria	Wien/Vienna	Belehrendes und Unterhaltendes	cultural paper
Austria	Wien/Vienna	Blätter für Theater, Musik und Kunst	fine arts paper

Country	Published at	Title	Notes
Austria	Wien/Vienna	Christlich-soziale Arbeiter-Zeitung	political paper
Austria	Wien/Vienna	Cook's-Welt-Reise-Zeitung	travel paper
Austria	Wien/Vienna	Cur-Liste Bad Ischl	lists guests at spa
Austria	Wien/Vienna	Das Panier des Fortschrittes	
Austria	Wien/Vienna	Das Vaterland	Austrian monarchy paper
Austria	Wien/Vienna	Das Wienerblättchen	
Austria	Wien/Vienna	Das Wort der Frau	women
Austria	Wien/Vienna	Das Zelt	Jewish
Austria	Wien/Vienna	Deborah	Jewish
Austria	Wien/Vienna	Der Adler	
Austria	Wien/Vienna	Der Alpenfreund	Alpine paper
Austria	Wien/Vienna	Der Architekt	architect's paper
Austria	Wien/Vienna	Der Bauernbündler	Lower Austria farm paper
Austria	Wien/Vienna	Der Bautechniker	construction paper
Austria	Wien/Vienna	Der Hausbesitzer/Hausherren Zeitung	homeowner paper
Austria	Wien/Vienna	Der Humorist	humor
Austria	Wien/Vienna	Der jüdische Arbeiter	Jewish political
Austria	Wien/Vienna	Der Kinobesitzer	movie theater paper
Austria	Wien/Vienna	Der neue Mahnruf	

Country	Published at	Title	Notes
Austria	Wien/Vienna	Der Omnibus	
Austria	Wien/Vienna	Der österreichische Zuschauer	
Austria	Wien/Vienna	Der Radikale	radical
Austria	Wien/Vienna	Der Schnee	seasonal Alpine paper
Austria	Wien/Vienna	Der Unpartheyische	independent political
Austria	Wien/Vienna	Der Wähler	political paper
Austria	Wien/Vienna	Der Wanderer	
Austria	Wien/Vienna	Deutsches Volksblatt	
Austria	Wien/Vienna	Deutsches Wochenblatt	
Austria	Wien/Vienna	Die Arbeit	labor paper
Austria	Wien/Vienna	Die Arbeiterin	women's labor paper
Austria	Wien/Vienna	Die Arbeiterinnen	women's labor paper
Austria	Wien/Vienna	Die Bombe	fashion paper
Austria	Wien/Vienna	Die Bühne	theater paper
Austria	Wien/Vienna	Die Debatte und Wiener Lloyd	
Austria	Wien/Vienna	Die Drogisten-Zeitung	pharmacist paper
Austria	Wien/Vienna	Die Fackel	society members
Austria	Wien/Vienna	Die Film-Welt	movie paper
Austria	Wien/Vienna	Die Kino-Woche	movie paper

Country	Published at	Title	Notes
Austria	Wien/Vienna	Die Lokomotive	locomotive industry
Austria	Wien/Vienna	Die Muskete	humor
Austria	Wien/Vienna	Die neue Welt	Jewish
Austria	Wien/Vienna	Die neue Zeitung	
Austria	Wien/Vienna	Die Neuzeit	
Austria	Wien/Vienna	Die Presse	press
Austria	Wien/Vienna	Die rote Fahne	Communist party paper
Austria	Wien/Vienna	Die Stimme [Alte Folge]	Jewish
Austria	Wien/Vienna	Die Stimme [Neue Folge]	Jewish
Austria	Wien/Vienna	Die Vedette	military paper
Austria	Wien/Vienna	Die Wählerin	women's political paper
Austria	Wien/Vienna	Die Wahrheit	Jewish
Austria	Wien/Vienna	Die Welt	Jewish
Austria	Wien/Vienna	Die Zeit	
Austria	Wien/Vienna	Dr. Blochs Österreichische Wochenschrift	Jewish
Austria	Wien/Vienna	Erdöl-Zeitung	petroleum paper
Austria	Wien/Vienna	Erste allgemeine öster. Hebammen-Zeitung	midwife paper
Austria	Wien/Vienna	Esra	Jewish academic paper
Austria	Wien/Vienna	Freie Tribüne	Jewish political

Country	Published at	Title	Notes
Austria	Wien/Vienna	Fremden-Blatt	tourist paper
Austria	Wien/Vienna	Fussball-Zeitung	soccer
Austria	Wien/Vienna	Gerichts-Halle	court paper
Austria	Wien/Vienna	Hebammen-Zeitung	midwife paper
Austria	Wien/Vienna	Illustriertes Familienblatt	
Austria	Wien/Vienna	Illustriertes Wiener Extrablatt	
Austria	Wien/Vienna	Illustrirte Monatshefte	Jewish
Austria	Wien/Vienna	Jahresbericht der Schulen des Frauenerwerb-Vereins	annual school report
Austria	Wien/Vienna	Jahresbericht des Mädchen-Lyzeums am Kohlmarkt	annual school report
Austria	Wien/Vienna	Jahresbericht des Vereins für erweiterte Frauenbildung in Wien	annual school report
Austria	Wien/Vienna	Jüdische Korrespondenz	Jewish
Austria	Wien/Vienna	Jüdische Volksstimme	Jewish
Austria	Wien/Vienna	Jüdische Zeitung	Jewish
Austria	Wien/Vienna	Jüdisches Volksblatt	Jewish
Austria	Wien/Vienna	Kalender und Jahrbuch für Israeliten	Jewish
Austria	Wien/Vienna	Kalender und Jahrbuch für Israeliten [II. Folge]	Jewish
Austria	Wien/Vienna	Kalender und Jahrbuch für Israeliten [III. Folge]	Jewish
Austria	Wien/Vienna	Kikirikij	humor

Country	Published at	Title	Notes
Austria	Wien/Vienna	Menorah	Jewish multilingual
Austria	Wien/Vienna	Militär-Zeitung	military paper
Austria	Wien/Vienna	Montags-Zeitung	
Austria	Wien/Vienna	Morgenpost	daily
Austria	Wien/Vienna	Nationalzeitung	Jewish
Austria	Wien/Vienna	Neu-ankommender Currier Auß Wienn	
Austria	Wien/Vienna	Neue Allgemeine Wiener Handlungs- und Industrie-Zeitung	business and industry paper
Austria	Wien/Vienna	Neue Folge der Gesundheits-Zeitung	health paper
Austria	Wien/Vienna	Neue Freie Presse	
Austria	Wien/Vienna	Neue Kino Rundschau	movie paper
Austria	Wien/Vienna	Neue Nationalzeitung	Jewish
Austria	Wien/Vienna	Neue Zeitung	Jewish
Austria	Wien/Vienna	Neues 8-Uhr Blatt	daily
Austria	Wien/Vienna	Neues Fremdenblatt	tourist paper
Austria	Wien/Vienna	Neues Wiener Journal	
Austria	Wien/Vienna	Neues Wiener Tagblatt	daily
Austria	Wien/Vienna	Oesterreichische Jugend-Zeitschrift	youth paper
Austria	Wien/Vienna	Österreichische Buchhändler-Korrespondenz	bookseller paper
Austria	Wien/Vienna	Österreichische Illustrirte Zeitung	

Country	Published at	Title	Notes
Austria	Wien/Vienna	Österreichische Lehrerinnen-Zeitung	female teachers
Austria	Wien/Vienna	Österreichische Nähmaschinen- und Fahrrad-Zeitung	sewing machine paper
Austria	Wien/Vienna	Österreichischer Beobachter	
Austria	Wien/Vienna	Österreichisches entomologisches Wochenblatt	entomology paper
Austria	Wien/Vienna	Österreichisches pädagogisches Wochenblatt	teachers
Austria	Wien/Vienna	Österreichisch-ungarisches Cantoren-Zeitung	Jewish cantor publication
Austria	Wien/Vienna	Politische Frauen-Zeitung	women's supplement
Austria	Wien/Vienna	Populäre österreichische Gesundheits-Zeitung	health paper
Austria	Wien/Vienna	Punch	humor
Austria	Wien/Vienna	Reichs-Gesetz-Blatt für das Kaiserthum Österreich	Austrian law paper
Austria	Wien/Vienna	Reichspost	
Austria	Wien/Vienna	Rohö Zeitung	women
Austria	Wien/Vienna	Schild und Schwert	
Austria	Wien/Vienna	Selbst-Emancipation	Jewish
Austria	Wien/Vienna	Social-politische Frauen-Zeitung	women's political paper
Austria	Wien/Vienna	Stenographische Protokolle der Verhandlungen der Zionisten-Kongresse	Jewish
Austria	Wien/Vienna	Süddeutscher Geschäftsanzeiger	business paper
Austria	Wien/Vienna	Union	insurance trade paper

Country	Published at	Title	Notes
Austria	Wien/Vienna	Unsere Tribüne	Jewish political
Austria	Wien/Vienna	Vaterländische Blätter für den österreichischen Kaiserstaat	Imperial paper
Austria	Wien/Vienna	Verlustliste	Austro-Hungary casualties
Austria	Wien/Vienna	Verlustliste Alphabetisches Verzeichnis	Austro-Hungary casualty index
Austria	Wien/Vienna	Volks-Zeitung	
Austria	Wien/Vienna	Wele-Neuigkeitsblatt	
Austria	Wien/Vienna	Wiener Allgemeine Zeitung	500 years U Heidelberg
Austria	Wien/Vienna	Wiener Bilder	pictorial
Austria	Wien/Vienna	Wiener Caricaturen	carkcatjres
Austria	Wien/Vienna	Wiener entomologische Zeitung	entomology
Austria	Wien/Vienna	Wiener Feuerwehrzeitung	fireman paper
Austria	Wien/Vienna	Wiener illustrirte Garten-Zeitung	
Austria	Wien/Vienna	Wiener Montagsjournal	
Austria	Wien/Vienna	Wiener Morgenzeitung	Jewish
Austria	Wien/Vienna	Wiener neueste Nachrichten	
Austria	Wien/Vienna	Wiener Zeitung	
Austria	Wien/Vienna	Wienerische Kirchenzeitung	Vienna church paper
Austria	Wien/Vienna	Wienerisches Diarium	

Country	Published at	Title	Notes
Austria	Wien/Vienna	Wochenschrift der K.K. Gesellschaft der Ärzte	physicians
Austria	Wien/Vienna	Wohlstand für Alle	anarchist paper
Austria	Wien/Vienna	Zeitschrift des Österreichischen Ingenieur-und Architekten-Vereins	construction paper
Austria	Wien/Vienna	Zeitschrift des Österreichischen Ingenieur-Vereins	construction paper
Austria	Wien/Vienna	Zeitung für Landwirtschaft	agricultural paper
Austria	Wiener Neustadt	Jahresbericht der Niederösterreichischen Ober-Realschule	annual school report
Austria	Znaim/Znojmo	Jahresbericht des Mädchen-Lyzeums der Stadt Znaim	annual school report
Austtia	Wien/Vienna	Das Fremden-Blatt	tourist paper
Belgium	Aalst	Der Landsturm	soldier paper WW I
Belgium	Arel/Arles	Areler Zeitung	wartime paper
Belgium	Brüssel/Brussels	Deutsche Brüsseler Zeitung	
Belgium	Malmedy	Organe Malmedy	mostly French; German ads
Belgium	St. Vith	Kreisblatt für den Kreis Malmedy	
Belgium	St. Vith	Malmedy-St. Vither Volkszeitung	
Belgium	St. Vith	St. Vither Volkszeitung	
Belgium	St. Vith	Wochenblatt für den Kreis Malmedy	
China	Shanghai	Shanghai Echo	
China	Tsientsin	Deutsch-chinesische Nachrichten	

Country	Published at	Title	Notes
China	Tsientsin	Deutsche Zeitung in Nordchina	
Crimea	Simferopol	Deutsche Zeitung für die Krim und Taurien	wartime paper
Croatia	Agram/Zagreb	Agramer Zeitung	
Croatia	Agram/Zagreb	Kroatischer Korrespondent	
Croatia	Brioni/Brijuni	Brioni Insel-Zeitung	
Croatia	Pola/Pula	Pola	southern Austria
Croatia	Pola/Pula	Polaer Tagblatt	
Croatia	Pola/Pula	Südösterreichische Nachrichten	
Croatia	Zagreb	Der Kroatische Korrespondent	
Czech Republic	Brünn/Brno	Brünner Hebammen-Zeitung	midwife paper
Czech Republic	Brünn/Brno	Brünner Tagesbote	Moravia
Czech Republic	Brünn/Brno	Deutsches Südmährisches Blatt	southern Moravia
Czech Republic	Brünn/Brno	Regierungsblatt für das Markgrafthum Mähren	Moravia; bilingual
Czech Republic	Brünn/Brno	Zeitschrift für die Geschichte der Juden in der Tschechoslowakei	Jewish Czech
Czech Republic	Budweis/České Budějovice	Südböhmische Volkszeitung	Bohemia
Czech Republic	Chomutov/Komotau	Allgemeine Feuerwehr-Zeitung	firemen's paper
Czech Republic	Eger/Cheb	Egere rAnzeiger	Bohemia
Czech Republic	Eger/Cheb	Egerer Zeitung	Bohemia

Country	Published at	Title	Notes
Czech Republic	Eger/Cheb	Unser Egerland	Bohemia
Czech Republic	Freiwaldau/Jesenik	Die Mährisch-Schlesische Presse	Moravia and Silesia
Czech Republic	Hohenelbe/Vrchlabi	Das Riesengebirge in Wort und Bild	travel publication
Czech Republic	Krumau/Český Krumlov	Böhmerwald Volksbote	political paper
Czech Republic	Mährisch Neustadt/Uničov	Nordmährische Rundschau	Moravia
Czech Republic	Mährisch Ostrau/Ostrava	Local-Anzeiger für Mähr.-Ostrau und Umgebung	Moravia
Czech Republic	Olmütz/Olomouc	Deutsches Nordmährerblatt	Moravia
Czech Republic	Olmütz/Olomouc	Mährisches Tagblatt	Moravia
Czech Republic	Pilsen/Plzeň	Jahresbericht des K. K. Gymnasiums zu Pilsen	annual school report
Czech Republic	Pilsen/Plzeň	Pilsner Tagblatt	Bohemia
Czech Republic	Prag/Prague	Bohemia	Bohemia
Czech Republic	Prag/Prague	Bohemia, ein Unterhaltungsblatt	literary
Czech Republic	Prag/Prague	Bohemia, oder Unterhaltungsblätter für gebildete Stände	literary
Czech Republic	Prag/Prague	Deutsche Zeitung Bohemia	
Czech Republic	Prag/Prague	Jahrbuch der Gesellschaft der Geschichte der Juden in der Čechoslowakischen Republik	Jewish in Czech area
Czech Republic	Prag/Prague	Landes-Gesetzblatt für das Königreich Böhmen	Bohemia; bilingual
Czech Republic	Prag/Prague	Landes-Regierungsblatt für das Königreich Böhmen	Bohemia; bilingual
Czech Republic	Prag/Prague	Prager Abendblatt	daily

Country	Published at	Title	Notes
Czech Republic	Prag/Prague	Zerztliche Correspondenz-Blatt für Böhmen	Bohemia medical
Czech Republic	Preßburg/Bratislava	Judaica	Jewish literary publication
Czech Republic	Preßburg/Bratislava	Pannonia	Slovakia
Czech Republic	Preßburg/Bratislava	Preßburger Zeitung	Slovakia
Czech Republic	Preßburg/Bratislava	Preßburgisches Wochenblatt	Slovakia
Czech Republic	Preßburg/Bratislava	Schrattenthals Frauenzeitung	women's paper
Czech Republic	Prossnitz/Prostějov	Prossnitzer Wochenblatt	Moravia
Czech Republic	Teplitz-Schönau/ Teplice-Šanov	Teplitz-Schönauer Anzeiger	Bohemia
Czech Republic	Troppau/Opava	Kais. Königl. Schlesische Troppauer Zeitung	Silesia
Czech Republic	Warnsdorf/Varnsdorf	Nordböhmisches Volksblatt	Bohemia
Czech Republic	Warnsdorf/Varnsdorf	Österreichische Volkszeitung	Bohemia
Czech Republic	Warnsdorf/Varnsdorf	Warnsdorfer Volkszeitung	Bohemia
Czech Republic	Wien/Vienna; Preßburg/ Bratislava	Jüdische Presse	Jewish
Czech Republic	Znaim/Znojmo	Znaimer Tagblatt	Moravia
Czech Republic	Znaim/Znojmo	Znaimer Wochenblatt	Moravia
Egypt	Cairo	Aegyptische Nachrichten	Moravia
England	London (etc)	Europe Speaks	exile papers; multilingual

Country	Published at	Title	Notes
Estonia	Dorpat/Tartu	Das Inland	Baltic region
Estonia	Dorpat/Tartu	Dörptsche Zeitung	Baltic region
Estonia	Tallinn/Reval	Revalsche Post-Zeitung	
France	war theatre	Armee-Zeitung der 2. Armee	wartime field paper
France	war theatre	Badener Lazarett-Zeitung	wartime field paper
France	war theatre	Daheim	wartime field paper
France	war theatre	Der Champagne-Kamerad	wartime field paper
France	war theatre	Die Mauer	wartime field paper
France	war theatre	Die Somme-Wacht	wartime field paper
France	war theatre	Die Wacht im Osten	wartime field paper
France	war theatre	Die Wacht im Westen	wartime field paper
France	war theatre	Düna-Zeitung	wartime field paper
France	war theatre	Gazette des Ardennes	wartime field paper
France	war theatre	Kriegs-Zeitung der Elften Armee	wartime field paper
France	war theatre	Kriegs-Zeitung für das XV. Armee-Korps	wartime field paper
France	war theatre	Landsturm	wartime field paper
France	war theatre	Landsturm's Krieg's Bote	wartime field paper
France	war theatre	Liller Kriegszeitung	wartime field paper
France	war theatre	Meldereiter im Sundgau	wartime field paper

Country	Published at	Title	Notes
France	war theatre	Seille-Bote	wartime field paper
France	war theatre	Unser Landsturm im Hennegau	wartime field paper
France	war theatre	Zwischen Maas und Mosel	wartime field paper
France	10th Army	Zeitung der 10. Armee	wartime field paper
France	14th Bayr. Armierungsbataillon	Der Armierer	wartime field paper
France	19th Res. Inf. Regt.	Die Sappe	wartime field paper
France	1st Bayr. Ersatz-Inf.-Regt.	Im Schützengraben in den Vogesen	wartime field paper
France	2nd Bayr. L. Esk.	Die Patrulle	wartime field paper
France	2nd Bayr. Landwehr-Inf.-Regt.	Der bayerische Landwehrmann	wartime field paper
France	2nd Bayr. Landwehr-Inf.-Regt.	Die bayerische Landwehr	wartime field paper
France	3rd Bayr. Landwehr-Inf.-Regt.	Der Drahtverhau	wartime field paper
France	6th Bayr. Landwehr-Division	Vogesenwacht	wartime field paper
France	7th Army	Kriegszeitung der 7. Armee	wartime field paper
France	8. Reserve-Korps	Chamlagne-Kriegs-Zeitung	wartime field paper
France	8th Bayr. Res. Div.	Schützengrabenzeitung	wartime field paper
France	Bapaume	Bapaumer Zeitung am Mittag	wartime field paper

Country	Published at	Title	Notes
France	Briey	Der Landsturm-Bote von Briey	wartime field paper
France	Champagne	Champagner Kriegs-Zeitung	wartime field paper
France	Gaede Abteilung, Logelbach	Bacillus verus	wartime field paper
France	Guebwiller/Gebweiler	Gebweilerer Wochenblatt	wartime; bilingual
France	Hagenau/Haguenau	Hagenauer Zeitung	Alsace
France	Hagenau/Haguenau	Unterländer Kurier	Alsace
France	Kolmar/Colmar	Elsässer Kurier	Alsace
France	Kolmar/Colmar	Elsässer Tagblatt	Alsace
France	Metz	Der Orientfrontkaempfer	military paper
France	Mülhausen/Mulhouse	Mülhauser Frauenzeitung	Alsace
France	Mülhausen/Mulhouse	Mülhauser Tagblatt	Alsace
France	Mülhausen/Mulhouse	Neue Mülhauser Zeitung	Alsace
France	Mülhausen/Mulhouse	Oberelsässische Landes-Zeitung	Alsace
France	Paris	Der Internationale Klassenkampf	Communist party paper
France	Schlettstadt/Séléstat	Schlettstadter Tageblatt	Alsace
France	St. Ludwig/Saint-Louis, France	Ober-Elsäßischer Volksfreund: Anzeiger für Hüningen, Sierenz und die angrenzenden Kantone	Sundgau Upper Alsace
France	Strasburg/Strasbourg	Central- und Bezirks-Amtsblatt für Elsass-Lothringen	Alsace-Lorraine

Country	Published at	Title	Notes
France	Strasburg/Strasbourg	Elsäss-Lothringisches Schulblatt	teacher paper
France	Strasburg/Strasbourg	La Tribune Juive (multilingual)	Jewish paper
France	Strasburg/Strasbourg	Le Juif (bilingual)	Jewish paper
France	Strasburg/Strasbourg	Niederrheinischer Kurier	
France	Strasburg/Strasbourg	Relation aller Fuernemmen und gedenckwuerdigen Historien	oldest newspaper in the world
France	Strasburg/Strasbourg	Strassburger Bürger-Zeitung	
France	Strasburg/Strasbourg	Strassburger Diözesanblatt	diocesan paper
France	Strasburg/Strasbourg	Straßburger Handelsblatt	business paper
France	Strasburg/Strasbourg	Strassburger neueste Nachrichten: General-Anzeiger für Strassburg und Elsass-Lothringen	Alsace-Lorraine
France	Strasburg/Strasbourg	Strassburger Post	
France	Strasburg/Strasbourg	Strassburger priveligierte Zeitung	
France	Strasburg/Strasbourg	Strassburgisches Wochenblatt	weekly; bilingual
France	Strasburg/Strasbourg	Weltbote	
France	Strasburg/Strasbourg	Zentral- und Bezirks Amtsblatt für Elsaß-Lothringen	Alsace-Lorraine
France	Württ. Gebirgsbattaillion	Der Horchposten des Kgl. Württembergischen Gebirgsbattaillions	wartime field paper
Georgia	Tiflis	Kaukasische Post	

Country	Published at	Title	Notes
Germany	Aachen/Aix-la-Chapelle	Aachener Wahrheits-Freund	Rhineland
Germany	Aachen/Aix-la-Chapelle	Amtsblatt der Regierung zu Aachen	Rhineland
Germany	Aachen/Aix-la-Chapelle	Echo der Gegenwart	500 years U Heidelberg
Germany	Aachen/Aix-la-Chapelle	Journal des Nieder- und Mittelrheins	Rhineland
Germany	Adenau	Adenauer Kreis- und Wochenblatt	Rhineland
Germany	Adenau	Kreis-Wochenblatt für den Kreis Adenau und Umgegend	Rhineland
Germany	Adenau	Wochenblatt für den Kreis Adenau und Umgegend	Rhineland
Germany	Ahrweiler	Ahrweiler Kreisblatt	Rhineland
Germany	Aichach	Amtsblatt für das Bezirksamts und Amtsgericht Aichach	Bavaria
Germany	Altenburg	Gnädigst privilegirtes Altenburgisches Intelligenz-Blatt	Thuringia
Germany	Altenburg	Zeitung für den deutschen Adel	nobility paper
Germany	Altona	Altonaer Nachrichten	Hamburg
Germany	Altona	Amtsblatt der Stadt Altona	Hamburg
Germany	Altona	Der Jude	Jewish
Germany	Altona	Schleswig-Holsteinische Provinzialblätter	Schleswig-Holstein
Germany	Amberg	Amberger Tagblatt	Bavaria
Germany	Amberg	Amberger Volkszeitung	Bavaria
Germany	Amberg	Jahresbericht über die Gewerbschule Amberg	school report
Germany	Amberg	Wochenblatt der Stadt Amberg	Bavaria

Country	Published at	Title	Notes
Germany	Ammendorf	Kriegs-Zeitung	wartime paper
Germany	Amorbach	Jahresbericht über die Fürstl.-Leining. Lateinschule zu Amorbach	school report
Germany	Andernach	Andernacher Burger-Blatt	Rhineland
Germany	Ansbach	Ansbacher Morgenblatt	Bavaria
Germany	Ansbach	Intelligenzblatt des Rezat-Kreises	Bavaria
Germany	Ansbach	Königlich Bayerisches Intelligenzblatt für Mittelfranken	Bavaria
Germany	Arnsberg	Amtsblatt für den Regierungs-Bezirk Arnsberg	Westphalia
Germany	Arnsberg	Arnsberger Intelligenz-Blatt	Westphalia
Germany	Arolsen/Bad Arolsen	Waldeckisches Intelligenz-Blatt	Waldeck
Germany	Arolsen/Bad Arolsen	Wöchentlich Oekonomisches Intelligenz-Blatt	Waldeck
Germany	Aschaffenburg	Aschaffenburger Wochenblatt	Bavaria
Germany	Aschaffenburg	Aschaffenburger Zeitung	Bavaria
Germany	Aschaffenburg	Herold des Glaubens	Bavaria
Germany	Aschaffenburg	Intelligenzblatt von Unterfranken und Aschaffenburg	Bavaria
Germany	Aschaffenburg	Königlich Bayerisches Kreis-Amtsblatt von Unterfranken und Aschaffenburg	Bavaria
Germany	Aschaffenburg	Neue Aschaffenburger Zeitung und Aschaffenburger Anzeiger	Bavaria
Germany	Augsburg	Allerneuestes Gradaus oder deutsches Volk	Bavaria

Country	Published at	Title	Notes
Germany	Augsburg	Allgemeine Zeitung	Bavaria
Germany	Augsburg	Augsburger Anzeigeblatt	Bavaria
Germany	Augsburg	Augsburger Neuester Nachrichten	Bavaria
Germany	Augsburg	Augsburger Post-Zeitung	Bavaria
Germany	Augsburg	Augsburger Sonntagsblatt	Bavaria
Germany	Augsburg	Augsburger Tagblatt	Bavaria
Germany	Augsburg	Augspurgische Ordinari Postzeitung	Bavaria
Germany	Augsburg	Der Hausfreund	Bavaria
Germany	Augsburg	Der Lechbote	Bavaria
Germany	Augsburg	Deutsches Wochenblatt für constitutionelle Monarchie	monarchy paper
Germany	Augsburg	Intelligenz-Blatt der königlichen Regierung von Schwaben und Neuburg	Bavaria
Germany	Augsburg	Intelligenz-Blatt und wöchentlicher Anzeiger der königlich bairischen Stadt Augsburg	Bavaria
Germany	Augsburg	Königlich Bayerisches Intelligenz-Blatt für den Ober-Donau Kreis	Bavaria
Germany	Augsburg	Neue Augsburger Zeitung	Bavaria
Germany	Augsburg	Tagblatt für die Kreishauptstadt Augsburg	Bavaria
Germany	Augsburg	Verhandlungen des Landraths im Ober-Donau Kreis	Bavaria
Germany	Aurich	Wöchentliche Ostfriesische Anzeigen und Nachrichten	East Frisia

Country	Published at	Title	Notes
Germany	Bamberg	Allgemeines Amtsblatt	Bavaria
Germany	Bamberg	Bamberger Journal	Bavaria
Germany	Bamberg	Bamberger Neueste Nachrichten	Bavaria
Germany	Bamberg	Bamberger Tagblatt	Bavaria
Germany	Bamberg	Der Freund der Wahrheit und des Volkes	Bavaria
Germany	Bamberg	Fränkischer Merkur	Bavaria
Germany	Bamberg	Tag-Blatt der Stadt Bamberg	Bavaria
Germany	Bamberg	Wöchentlicher Anzeiger für die katholische Geistichkeit	Catholic clergy
Germany	Barmen	Barmer Wochenblatt	Rhineland
Germany	Barmen	Barmer Zeitung	500 years U Heidelberg
Germany	Barmen	Jahresbericht über die Realschule Barmen	school report
Germany	Bayreuth	Bayreuther Intelligenz-Zeitung	Bavaria
Germany	Bayreuth	Bayreuther Zeitung	Bavaria
Germany	Bayreuth	Deutsche Reichs- und Gesetz-Zeitung	Bavaria
Germany	Bayreuth	Die braune Sonntagszeitung	National Socialist paper
Germany	Bayreuth	Fränkische Provinzialblätter	Bavaria
Germany	Bayreuth	Königlich bayerisches Intelligenz-Blatt für Oberfranken	Bavaria
Germany	Bayreuth	Sinai	Jewish paper
Germany	Bayreuth	Sudetendeutsche Zeitung	Sudetenland

Country	Published at	Title	Notes
Germany	Bayreuth	Sudetenland	Sudetenland Germans
Germany	Bensberg	Bensberger Volkszeitung	Rhineland
Germany	Bensberg	Bensberg-Gladbacher Anzeiger	Rhineland
Germany	Bensheim	Bergsträßer Anzeigeblatt	Hesse
Germany	Bergisch-Gladbach	Bergische Wacht	Rhineland
Germany	Bergisch-Gladbach	Bergisch-Gladbacher Volkszeitung	Rhineland
Germany	Bergisch-Gladbach	Rheinisch-Bergische Zeitung	Rhineland
Germany	Bergisch-Gladbach	Volksblatt für Bergisch-Gladbach und Umgegend	Rhineland
Germany	Berlin	Allgemeine deutsche Gärtnerzeitung	gardener paper
Germany	Berlin	Allgemeine Militär-Zeitung	Brandenburg
Germany	Berlin	Allgemeine preußische Staats-Zeitung	Brandenburg
Germany	Berlin	Allgemeine Uhrmacher-Zeitung	clockmaker paper
Germany	Berlin	Amtsblatt der deutschen Reichs-Postverwaltung	Brandenburg
Germany	Berlin	Amtsblatt der königlichen Regierung zu Berlin	Brandenburg
Germany	Berlin	Amtsblatt des preußischen Post-Departements	Prussia
Germany	Berlin	Arbeiterwohlfahrt	labor paper
Germany	Berlin	Arbeiter-Zeitung für Schlesien und Oberschlesien	Communist paper
Germany	Berlin	Aufwärts	youth trade newspaper
Germany	Berlin	Bar Kochba	Jewish

Country	Published at	Title	Notes
Germany	Berlin	Beiblatt der Freisinnigen Zeitung	500 years U Heidelberg
Germany	Berlin	Berichte für die Lehranstalt für die Wissenschaft des Judentums	Jewish
Germany	Berlin	Berliner Börsen-Courier	500 years U Heidelberg
Germany	Berlin	Berliner Börsen-Zeitung	stock market paper
Germany	Berlin	Berliner Courier	500 years U Heidelberg
Germany	Berlin	Berliner Gerichts-Zeitung	judicial newspaper
Germany	Berlin	Berliner Krakehler	humor
Germany	Berlin	Berliner Morgenpost	Brandenburg
Germany	Berlin	Berliner Tageblatt und Handels-Zeitung	Brandenburg
Germany	Berlin	Berliner Vereinsbote	Jewish
Germany	Berlin	Berliner Volks-Zeitung	Brandenburg
Germany	Berlin	Berliner Zeitung	DDR paper
Germany	Berlin	Berlinische Nachrichten von Staats- und gelehrten Sachen	Berlin
Germany	Berlin	Berlinische privilierte Zeitung	Brandenburg
Germany	Berlin	Berlinisches litterarisches Wochenblatt	literary
Germany	Berlin	Betriebsräte-Zeitschrift des DMV	metal worker paper
Germany	Berlin	Blau-Weiß-Blätter	Jewish hiking paper
Germany	Berlin	Blau-Weiß-Blätter (Neue Folge)	Jewish hiking paper

Country	Published at	Title	Notes
Germany	Berlin	Blau-Weiß-Blätter Führerheft	Jewish hiking paper
Germany	Berlin	Botanische Zeitung	botany
Germany	Berlin	Cameralistische Zeitung	German government
Germany	Berlin	Centralblatt der Bauverwaltung	building industry paper
Germany	Berlin	Central-Blatt für das deutsche Reich	German government
Germany	Berlin	Central-Verein Zeitung	Jewish
Germany	Berlin	Constitutionelle Zeitung	extra
Germany	Berlin	Das Echo	political
Germany	Berlin	Das Kleine Journal	
Germany	Berlin	Das neue Reich	
Germany	Berlin	Das Recht der Feder	literary
Germany	Berlin	Das rote Berlin	
Germany	Berlin	Der Brummbär	Brandenburg
Germany	Berlin	Der Bureauangestellte	office worker paper
Germany	Berlin	Der Demokrat	supplement
Germany	Berlin	Der freie Angestellte	employees paper
Germany	Berlin	Der Funke	Socialist daily
Germany	Berlin	Der jüdische Student	Jewish student publication
Germany	Berlin	Der jüdische Student (Neue Folge)	Jewish student publication

45

Country	Published at	Title	Notes
Germany	Berlin	Der jüdische Wille (Alte Folge)	Jewish
Germany	Berlin	Der jüdische Wille (Neue Folge)	Jewish
Germany	Berlin	Der junge Jude	Jewish youth publication
Germany	Berlin	Der Kämpfer	
Germany	Berlin	Der Kampfruf	
Germany	Berlin	Der Morgen	Jewish
Germany	Berlin	Der Papierfabrikant	papermaker weekly
Germany	Berlin	Der preußische Staatsanzeiger	Brandenburg
Germany	Berlin	Der Stahlhelm	
Germany	Berlin	Der Tagesspiegel	Brandenburg
Germany	Berlin	Deutsche Bau-Zeitung	construction paper
Germany	Berlin	Deutsche Fleischbeschauer-Zeitung	German meat inspector
Germany	Berlin	Deutsche Gemeinde-Zeitung	municipalities paper
Germany	Berlin	Deutsche Kolonialzeitung	German colonial paper
Germany	Berlin	Deutsche Schriftsteller-Zeitung	paper for authors
Germany	Berlin	Deutsche Uhrmacher-Zeitung	clockmaker paper
Germany	Berlin	Deutscher Reichs-Anzeiger	Brandenburg
Germany	Berlin	Deutsches Kolonialblatt	German colony administration
Germany	Berlin	Deutsches Tageblatt	500 years U Heidelberg

Country	Published at	Title	Notes
Germany	Berlin	Die Arbeit	trade union paper
Germany	Berlin	Die Deutsche Zucker-Industrie: Wochenblatt	sugar industry
Germany	Berlin	Die Feder	for authors and journalists
Germany	Berlin	Die Kämpferin	Communist party paper
Germany	Berlin	Die KPD	
Germany	Berlin	Die Kreatur	Jewish
Germany	Berlin	Die literarische Praxis	literary
Germany	Berlin	Die Post aus Deutschland	Voss
Germany	Berlin	Die Redaktion	literary
Germany	Berlin	Die Rote Front	
Germany	Berlin	Die Schwarze Fahne	
Germany	Berlin	Die Schwarze Front	
Germany	Berlin	Die Voss	Brandenburg
Germany	Berlin	Dramaturgisches Wochenblatt	teacher paper
Germany	Berlin	Eiserne Front	
Germany	Berlin	Garten-Zeitung	gardener paper
Germany	Berlin	Germania	500 years U Heidelberg
Germany	Berlin	Gewissen	journalism
Germany	Berlin	Hausangestellten-Zeitung	domestic worker paper

Country	Published at	Title	Notes
Germany	Berlin	Im Deutschen Reich	Jewish
Germany	Berlin	Israelitische Rundschau	Jewish
Germany	Berlin	Jahrbuch für jüdische Geschichte und Literatur	Jewish literary publication
Germany	Berlin	Jeschurun (Neue Folge)	Jewish
Germany	Berlin	Jüdische Arbeits- und Wanderfürsorge	Jewish
Germany	Berlin	Jüdische Rundschau	Jewish
Germany	Berlin	Kameralistische Zeitung	government paper
Germany	Berlin	Kampfsignal	
Germany	Berlin	Kartell-Convent Blätter	Jewish
Germany	Berlin	Kartell-Mitteilungen	Jewish
Germany	Berlin	Kladderadatsch	satire
Germany	Berlin	Königlich preußische Staats-Anzeiger	Brandenburg
Germany	Berlin	Königlich preußisches Central-Polizei-Blatt	Brandenburg
Germany	Berlin	Königlich privilegirte Berlinische Zeitung von Staats- und gelehrten Sachen	Brandenburg
Germany	Berlin	Kyffhäuser	military veteran paper
Germany	Berlin	Linnaea	botany
Germany	Berlin	Locomotive	political
Germany	Berlin	Magazin für die Wissenschaft des Judentums	Jewish

48

Country	Published at	Title	Notes
Germany	Berlin	Medizinische Zeitung	medical paper
Germany	Berlin	Militär-Wochenblatt	military paper
Germany	Berlin	Militär-Zeitung	military paper
Germany	Berlin	Mitteilungen aus dem Verband der Vereine für jüdische Geschichte und Literatur in Deutschland	Jewish
Germany	Berlin	Mitteilungen der Arbeitsgemeinschaft jüdisch-liberale Jugendvereine Deutschlands	Jewish youth publication
Germany	Berlin	Mitteilungen der Gesellschaft für jüdische Volkskunde [Neue Folge]	Jewish
Germany	Berlin	Mitteilungsblatt der Arbeitsgemeinschaft freier Angestelltenverbände	employees union paper
Germany	Berlin	Montagspost	
Germany	Berlin	Nachrichtendienst	Jewish
Germany	Berlin	National-Zeitung	500 years U Heidelberg
Germany	Berlin	National-Zeitung	Brandenburg
Germany	Berlin	Neue jüdische Monatshefte	Jewish
Germany	Berlin	Neue Mannigfaltigkeiten	
Germany	Berlin	Neue preußische Zeitung	500 years U Heidelberg
Germany	Berlin	Neue preußische Zeitung	Brandenburg
Germany	Berlin	Neue Zeit	CDU paper in DDR

Country	Published at	Title	Notes
Germany	Berlin	Neues Deutschland	official paper in DDR (SED)
Germany	Berlin	Neueste Mittheilungen	Prussian official press
Germany	Berlin	Norddeutsche Allgemeine Zeitung	500 years U Heidelberg
Germany	Berlin	Norddeutsche allgemeine Zeitung	Brandenburg
Germany	Berlin	Ost und West	Jewish
Germany	Berlin	Palästina	Jewish
Germany	Berlin	Palästina Nachrichten	Jewish
Germany	Berlin	Permanente Revolution	
Germany	Berlin	Protestantische Kirchenzeitung	500 years U Heidelberg
Germany	Berlin	Provinzial-Correspondenz	Prussian official press
Germany	Berlin	Reichswart	political
Germany	Berlin	Rundschau der Frau	women's labor paper
Germany	Berlin	Sattler- und Portefeuiller Zeitung	saddler paper
Germany	Berlin	Sattler- und Tapezierer Zeitung	saddler paper
Germany	Berlin	Sattler-Tapezierer- und Portefeuiller Zeitung	saddler paper
Germany	Berlin	Sattler-Zeitung	saddler paper
Germany	Berlin	Sichel und Hammer	Communist
Germany	Berlin	Solidarität	labor paper
Germany	Berlin	Sonntagsblatt	religious paper

Country	Published at	Title	Notes
Germany	Berlin	Tägliche Rundschau	500 years U Heidelberg
Germany	Berlin	Tribunal	
Germany	Berlin	Ulk	satire
Germany	Berlin	Volk und Land	Jewish political
Germany	Berlin	Volks-Zeitung	Brandenburg
Germany	Berlin	Vossische Zeitung	Brandenburg
Germany	Berlin	Zeitbilder	a Voss paper
Germany	Berlin	Zeitschrift für Demographie und Statistik der Juden [Alte Folge]	Jewish statistics
Germany	Berlin	Zeitschrift für Demographie und Statistik der Juden [Neue Folge]	Jewish statistics
Germany	Berlin	Zeitschrift für die Wissenschaft der Juden	Jewish
Germany	Berlin	Zeitung des Vereins deutscher Eisenbahn-Verwaltungen	railroad administration
Germany	Berlin	Zion	Jewish
Germany	Berlin; Leipzig	Korrespondent für Deutschlands Buchdrucker und Schriftgießer	labor paper
Germany	Berlin; Wien/Vienna	Der Jude	Jewish
Germany	Berlin-Charlottenburg	Der Judenkenner	anti-Semitic
Germany	Berlinchen	General-Anzeiger für Berlinchen, Bernstein und Umgegend	Brandenburg
Germany	Berlin-Neukölln	Neubau und Siedlung	

Country	Published at	Title	Notes
Germany	Bieberach	Wochenblatt für Papierfabrikation	papermaker weekly
Germany	Bielefeld	Jahresbericht über das Schuljahr 1873–1874	school report
Germany	Bingen	Intelligenzblatt für den Kreis Bingen	Hesse
Germany	Bingen	Rhein- und Nahe-Zeitung	Hesse
Germany	Birkenfeld	Amtsblatt für den Landesteil Birkenfeld	Rhineland
Germany	Bitburg	Bitburger Kreis- und Intelligenzblatt	Rhineland
Germany	Blieskastel	Jahresbericht über die lateinische Schule Blieskastel	school report
Germany	Bochum	Bochumer Kreisblatt	Westphalia
Germany	Bockenheim	Bockenheimer Anzeiger	Frankfurt am Main
Germany	Bockenheim	Frankfurt-Bockenheimer Anzeige-Blatt	Frankfurt am Main
Germany	Bonn	Allgemeiner Bonner Anzeiger für Industrie, Handel und Gewerbe	Rhineland
Germany	Bonn	Annalen	Rhineland
Germany	Bonn	Beiträge zur Ausbreitung nützlicher Kenntnisse	Rhineland
Germany	Bonn	Blätter für religiöse Erziehung	religious paper
Germany	Bonn	Bonner Anzeiger	Rhineland
Germany	Bonn	Bonner Chronik	Rhineland
Germany	Bonn	Bonner Dekadenschrift	Rhineland
Germany	Bonn	Bonner Tageblatt	Rhineland

Country	Published at	Title	Notes
Germany	Bonn	Bonner Volksblatt	Rhineland
Germany	Bonn	Bonner Volkszeitung	Rhineland
Germany	Bonn	Bonner Wochenblatt	Rhineland
Germany	Bonn	Bonner Zeitung	Rhineland
Germany	Bonn	Bönnischer Sitten, Staats- und Geschichtslehrer	Rhineland
Germany	Bonn	Bönnisches Wochenblatt	Rhineland
Germany	Bonn	Deutsche demokratische Zeitung	Rhineland
Germany	Bonn	Feuilles d'affiches annonces et avis divers de Bonn	Rhineland; bilingual
Germany	Bonn	Gnädigst privilegies Bönnisches Intelligenz-Blatt	Rhineland
Germany	Bonn	Mittelrheinische Landeszeitung	Rhineland
Germany	Bonn	Neue Bonner Zeitung	Rhineland
Germany	Bonn	Rheinische Allgemeine Zeitung	Rhineland
Germany	Bonn	Spartacus	Rhineland; political
Germany	Bonn	Volksblatt für die Kreise Bonn und Sieg	Rhineland
Germany	Bonn	Volksmund	Rhineland
Germany	Bonn	Wochenblatt des Bönnischen Bezirks	Rhineland
Germany	Braunschweig	Braunschweigische landwirtschaftliche Zeitung	agricultural paper
Germany	Braunschweig	Naturwissenschaftliche Rundschau	science

Country	Published at	Title	Notes
Germany	Braunschweig	Zeitschrift für die Geschichte der Juden in Deutschland	Jewish history
Germany	Bremen	Bremer Zeitung	
Germany	Bremen	Deutsche Auswanderer-Zeitung	emigration paper
Germany	Bremen	Milchwirtschaftliches Zentralblatt	dairy paper
Germany	Bremen	Weser-Zeitung	
Germany	Brünsbüttel	Kanal-Zeitung	Schleswig-Holstein canal paper
Germany	Bückeburg	Anzeigen des Fürstenthums Schaumburg-Lippe	Schaumburg-Lippe
Germany	Buckow	Buckower Local-Anzeiger	Brandenburg
Germany	Budissen	Budissener Nachrichten	Saxony
Germany	Burghausen	Jahresbericht über die kgl. Bayerische Studienanstalt in Burghausen	school report
Germany	Bütow	Bütower Anzeiger	Brandenburg
Germany	Cassel/Kassel	Casselische Polizey- und Commerzien-Zeitung	Hesse
Germany	Celle	Jahresbericht über das Gymnasium Celle	school report
Germany	Charlottenburg	Charlottenburger Zeitung	Berlin
Germany	Charlottenburg	Kornblumen	Sunday supplement
Germany	Chemnitz	Die Spinnmaschine	
Germany	Chemnitz; Leipzig	Deutsche Industri-Zeitung	industry paper
Germany	Coburg	Bayerische Ostmark Coburger National-Zeitung	Bavaria

54

Country	Published at	Title	Notes
Germany	Coburg	Coburger Nationalzeitung	Bavaria
Germany	Coburg	Coburger Regierungs-Blatt	Bavaria
Germany	Coburg	Coburger Regierungs-Blatt / Bezirksamt Coburg	Bavaria
Germany	Coburg	Coburger Zeitung	Bavaria and Saxony
Germany	Coburg	Coburgische wöchentliche Anzeige	Bavaria and Saxony
Germany	Coburg	Herzogl. Sachsen-Coburgisches Regierungs- und Intelligenzblatt	Bavaria and Saxony
Germany	Coburg	Herzogl. Sachsen-Coburg-Saalfeldes Regierungs- und Intelligenzblatt	Bavaria and Saxony
Germany	Coburg	Regierungs-Blatt für das Herzogtum Coburg	Bavaria and Saxony
Germany	Cochem	Cochemer Anzeiger	Rhineland
Germany	Cöthen/Koethen	Chemische Zeitung	chemical paper
Germany	Dachau	Amper-Bote	Bavaria
Germany	Darmstadt	Allgemeine Kirchenzeitung	church paper
Germany	Darmstadt	Amtsblatt der großherzoglichen Oberstudiendirektion	Hesse school council
Germany	Darmstadt	Amtsblatt des großherzoglichen Ministerium der Finanzen	Hesse finance ministry
Germany	Darmstadt	Amtsblatt des großherzoglichen Oberschulraths	Hesse school council
Germany	Darmstadt	Darmstädter Freie Presse	Hesse
Germany	Darmstadt	Darmstädter Tageblatt	500 years U Heidelberg
Germany	Darmstadt	Darmstädter Zeitung	Hesse

Country	Published at	Title	Notes
Germany	Darmstadt	Hessische landwirtschaftliche Zeitschrift	agricultural paper
Germany	Darmstadt	Illustriertes Unterhaltungs-Blatt	Hesse entertainment section
Germany	Darmstadt	Intelligenzblatt für die Provinz Oberhessen	Friedberg Hesse area
Germany	Darmstadt	Lauterbacher Anzeiger	Lauterbach Hesse area
Germany	Darmstadt	Neue Militär-Zeitung	Hesse
Germany	Darmstadt	Neuer Anzeiger	Hesse
Germany	Darmstadt	Oberhessische Volkszeitung	Alsfeld Hesse area
Germany	Darmstadt	Wochenbeilage der Darmstädter Zeitung	Hesse
Germany	Deggendorf	Deggendorfer Donaubote	Bavaria
Germany	Dermold	Die Wage	Lippe
Germany	Deßau/Dessau	Der preußische Postfreund für Norddeutschland	postal paper
Germany	Deßau/Dessau	Sulamith	Jewish
Germany	Detmold	Fürstlich-Lippisches Regierungs- und Anzeigeblatt	Lippe
Germany	Detmold	Lippische Landes-Zeitung	500 years U Heidelberg
Germany	Detmold	Lippisches Volksblatt	Lippe
Germany	Detmold	Westfälisch-Schaumburgische Zeitung	500 years U Heidelberg
Germany	Dillingen	Jahresbericht von der Königlichen Studien-Anstalt zu Dillingen	school report
Germany	Dillingen	Tagblatt für die Städte Dillingen, Lauingen, Höchstadt, Wertingen und Gundelfingen	Bavaria

Country	Published at	Title	Notes
Germany	Dillingen	Wochenblatt der Stadt Dillingen	Bavaria
Germany	Dinkelsbühl	Dinkelsbühlisches Intelligenzblatt	Bavaria
Germany	Dortmund	Amtsblatt für die Provinz Westfalen	Westphalia
Germany	Dresden	Abend-Zeitung	Saxony
Germany	Dresden	Amtsblatt der königlichen Direktion der sächsischen Eisenbahnen	Saxony
Germany	Dresden	Betriebsgemeinschaft Renner	
Germany	Dresden	Der Calculator an der Elbe	Saxony
Germany	Dresden	Der Freiheitskampf	Saxony
Germany	Dresden	Der letzte Appell	
Germany	Dresden	Der Sonntag	
Germany	Dresden	Dresdner Anzeiger	500 years U Heidelberg
Germany	Dresden	Dresdner Journal	500 years U Heidelberg
Germany	Dresden	Dresdner Journal	Saxony
Germany	Dresden	Dresdner Morgenzeitung	Saxony
Germany	Dresden	Dresdner Nachrichten	500 years U Heidelberg
Germany	Dresden	Dresdner Zeitung	500 years U Heidelberg
Germany	Dresden	Dresdner Zeitung	Saxony
Germany	Dresden	Monatsschrift für Geschichte und Wissenschaft des Judentums	Jewish

Country	Published at	Title	Notes
Germany	Dresden	Spartakus	
Germany	Dresden	Wochenblatt	Saxony agricultural paper
Germany	Dresden	Wöchentlicher Anzeiger	Saxony
Germany	Duisburg	Duisburger Intelligenz-Zeitung	Rhineland
Germany	Duisburg	Jahresbericht über das Königliche Gymnasium zu Duisburg	Rhineland
Germany	Düren	Dürener Anzeiger und Unterhaltungsblatt	Rhineland
Germany	Düren	Dürener Zeitung	Rhineland
Germany	Düren	General-Anzeiger für Stadt und Kreis Düren	Rhineland
Germany	Dürkheim/Bad Dürkheim	Jahresbericht über die Lateinische Schule zu Dürkheim	school report
Germany	Dürkheim/Bad Dürkheim	Wöchentliches Unterhaltungs-Blatt für den Kanton Dürkheim	Bavarian Palatinate
Germany	Düsseldorf	Amtsblatt für den Regierungsbezirk Düsseldorf	Rhineland
Germany	Düsseldorf	Bergischer Türmer	Rhineland
Germany	Düsseldorf	Düsseldorfer Erzähler	Rhineland
Germany	Düsseldorf	Düsseldorfer Intelligenz- und Adreß-Blatt	Rhineland
Germany	Düsseldorf	Düsseldorfer Literarisch-Merkantilisches Intelligenz- und Adreß-Blatt	Rhineland
Germany	Düsseldorf	Düsseldorfer Zeitung	500 years U Heidelberg
Germany	Düsseldorf	Gülich und bergische wöchentliche Nachrichten	Rhineland
Germany	Düsseldorf	Jüdische Allgemeine	Jewish

Country	Published at	Title	Notes
Germany	Düsseldorf	Königliches Düsseldorfer Intelligenzblatt	Rhineland
Germany	Düsseldorf	Rheinisches Land	Rhineland tourism
Germany	Edenkoben	Jahresbericht über die kgl. Bayerische Studienanstalt in Edenkoben	school report
Germany	Ehrenbreitstein	Allgemeines Intelligenzblatt für die Fürstlich-Nassau-Weilburgischen und Nassau-Sayn-Hachenburgischen Lande	Rhineland
Germany	Ehrenbreitstein	Ehrenbreitsteiner Intelligenzblatt	Rhineland
Germany	Eichstätt	Eichstätter Intelligenzblatt	Bavaria
Germany	Eichstätt	Eichstätter Tagblatt	Bavaria
Germany	Eisenach	Stimme der Kirche	religious paper
Germany	Eisenberg	Eisenbergisches Nachrichtenblatt	Saxony
Germany	Eisenstadt	Burgenländische Freiheit	Burgenland
Germany	Eisleben	Jahresbericht von Ostern 1863 bis dahin 1864 (Gymnasium Eisleben)	Saxony-Anhalt
Germany	Elberfeld	Conservative Provinzial-Zeitung für Rheinland und Westphalen	Rhineland
Germany	Elberfeld	Elberfelder Intelligenzblatt	Rhineland
Germany	Elberfeld	Elberfelder Zeitung	500 years U Heidelberg
Germany	Elberfeld	Rheinisches conservatives Volksblatt	Rhineland
Germany	Ellrich	Journal von und für Deutschland	Thuringia

59

Country	Published at	Title	Notes
Germany	Ellwangen	Königlich Württembergisches Allgemeines Amts- und Intelligenz-Blatt für den Jaxt-Kreis	Württemberg
Germany	Engelskirchen	Bergische Wacht	Rhineland
Germany	Erfurt	Amtsblatt der Königlichen Regierung zu Erfurt	Thuringia
Germany	Erfurt	Erfurtisches Intelligenz-Blatt	Thuringia
Germany	Erfurt	Möllers deutsche Gärtner-Zeitung	gardener paper
Germany	Erfurt	Neues Journal für die Botanik	botany
Germany	Erfurt	Regierungsblatt für das Land Thüringen	Thuringia
Germany	Erfurt	Regierungsblatt für Thüringen	Thuringia
Germany	Erlangen	Allgemeiner Kameral-, Oekonomie-, Forst- und Technologie-Korrespondent	Bavaria
Germany	Erlangen	Erlanger Mittwochs-Blatt	Bavaria
Germany	Erlangen	Erlanger Real-Zeitung	Bavaria
Germany	Erlangen	Erlanger Tagblatt	Bavaria
Germany	Erlangen	Erlanger Zeitung	Bavaria
Germany	Erlangen	Jahresbericht der lateinischen Vorbereitungsschulen zu Erlangen	Bavaria
Germany	Eschweiler; Berlin-Steglitz	Die Freistatt	Jewish cultural paper
Germany	Essen & Dortmund	Rheinisch Westfälische Zeitung	500 years U Heidelberg
Germany	Euskirchen	Erfa, Kreis-Intelligenzblatt für Euskirchen, Rheinbach und Ahrweiler	Rhineland

Country	Published at	Title	Notes
Germany	Eutin	Ostholsteinischer Anzeiger	Schleswig-Holstein
Germany	Fehrbellin	Fehrbelliner Zeitung	agricultural
Germany	Flörsheim	Flörsheimer Zeitung	Hesse
Germany	Forchheim	Amtsblatt für die königlichen Bezirksämter Forchheim und Ebermannstadt	Bavaria
Germany	Frankenthal	Frankenthaler Wochen-Blatt	Bavarian Palatinate
Germany	Frankenthal	Jahresbericht über die Königliche Bayerische Lateinische Schule . . . Frankenthal	annual school report
Germany	Frankfurt am Main	Amts-Blatt der freien Stadt Frankfurt	Frankfurt
Germany	Frankfurt am Main	Amtsblatt für den Stadtkreis Frankfurt a. M.	
Germany	Frankfurt am Main	Anzeigeblatt der städtischen Behörden zu Frankfurt am Main	
Germany	Frankfurt am Main	Badener Lazarett-Zeitung	war hospital paper
Germany	Frankfurt am Main	Central-Anzeiger für jüdische Literatur	Jewish literary paper
Germany	Frankfurt am Main	Das illustrierte Blatt	
Germany	Frankfurt am Main	Der israelitische Volkslehrer	Jewish
Germany	Frankfurt am Main	Der teutsche Reichs-Herold	
Germany	Frankfurt am Main	Diarium Hebdomadale, oder wöchentliche auiso	
Germany	Frankfurt am Main	Die Fackel	
Germany	Frankfurt am Main	Frankfurter Aerzte-Correspondenz	physicians

61

Country	Published at	Title	Notes
Germany	Frankfurt am Main	Frankfurter Bürgerzeitung Sonne	
Germany	Frankfurt am Main	Frankfurter Illustrierte	Hesse
Germany	Frankfurt am Main	Frankfurter Israelitisches Familienblatt	Jewish
Germany	Frankfurt am Main	Frankfurter Journal	500 years U Heidelberg
Germany	Frankfurt am Main	Frankfurter Konversationsblatt	
Germany	Frankfurt am Main	Frankfurter Nachrichten	
Germany	Frankfurt am Main	Frankfurter Nachrichten und Intelligenzblatt	
Germany	Frankfurt am Main	Frankfurter Oberpostamts-Zeitung	postal paper
Germany	Frankfurt am Main	Frankfurter Universitäts-Zeitung	university paper
Germany	Frankfurt am Main	Frankfurter Zeitung	500 years U Heidelberg
Germany	Frankfurt am Main	Frankfurter Zeitung und Handelsblatt	
Germany	Frankfurt am Main	Gemeindeblatt der Israelitischen Gemeinde Frankfurt am Main	Jewish congregational paper
Germany	Frankfurt am Main	Hessisch-Nassauischer Volksbote	
Germany	Frankfurt am Main	Intelligenz-Blatt der freien Stadt Frankfurt	Frankfurt
Germany	Frankfurt am Main	Israelitische Annalen	Jewish
Germany	Frankfurt am Main	Israelitische Religionsgesellschaft Frankfurt a.M.	Jewish
Germany	Frankfurt am Main	Jahrbuch der Jüdisch-Literarischen Gesellschaft	Jewish literary publication
Germany	Frankfurt am Main	Jahrbücher für jüdische Geschichte und Literatur	Jewish literary publication
Germany	Frankfurt am Main	Jeschurun (Alte Folge)	Jewish

Country	Published at	Title	Notes
Germany	Frankfurt am Main	Jüdische Zeitschrift für Wissenschaft und Leben	Jewish
Germany	Frankfurt am Main	Kleine Presse	
Germany	Frankfurt am Main	Korrespondenzblatt des Vereins zur Gründung und Erhaltung einer Akademie für die Wissenschaft des Judentums	Jewish
Germany	Frankfurt am Main	Liberales Judentum	Jewish
Germany	Frankfurt am Main	Medizinisches Wochenblatt	medical
Germany	Frankfurt am Main	Mitteldeutsche Rundschau	
Germany	Frankfurt am Main	Nachalath Zewi	Jewish
Germany	Frankfurt am Main	Neueste preußische Zeitung	
Germany	Frankfurt am Main	Neueste Zeitung	
Germany	Frankfurt am Main	Öffentlicher Anzeiger: Amtsblatt für den Stadtkreis Frankfurt a. M.	
Germany	Frankfurt am Main	Ordentliche wöchentliche Franckfurter Frag- und Anzeigungs-Nachrichten	
Germany	Frankfurt am Main	Philanthropin	Jewish school publication
Germany	Frankfurt am Main	Populär-wissenschaftliche Monatsblätter zur Belehrung über das Judentum für Gebildete aller Confessionen	Jewish
Germany	Frankfurt am Main	Sonntagsgruß: Kirchlicher Anzeiger für Frankfurt a.M. und Umgebung	religious paper
Germany	Frankfurt am Main	Wissenschaftliche Zeitschrift für jüdische Theologie	Jewish theology

Country	Published at	Title	Notes
Germany	Frankfurt am Main	Wochenblatt der Frankfurter Zeitung	
Germany	Frankfurt am Main	Zeitung des Großherzogthums Frankfurt	
Germany	Frankfurt am Main and Leipzig	Didaskalia: Blätter für Geist, Gemüth und Publizität	literary
Germany	Frankfurt an der Oder	Amtsblatt der Regierung zu Frankfurt an der Oder	Brandenburg
Germany	Frankfurt an der Oder	Dibre Emeth	Christian paper for Jewish readers
Germany	Frauendorf	Allgemeine deutsche Garten-Zeitung	gardener paper
Germany	Frauendorf	Bauern-Zeitung aus Frauendorf	farm paper
Germany	Freiberg	Berg- und Hüttenmännische Zeitung	miner paper; Saxony
Germany	Freiburg	Freiburger Wochenblatt	Baden
Germany	Freiburg	Freiburger Zeitung und Anzeiger für die westliche Schweiz	Baden
Germany	Freiburg	Großherzoglich badisches Amts- und Regierungsblatt für den Oberrhein-Kreis	Baden laws and regulations
Germany	Freiburg	Notariatsblatt für das Großherzogthum Baden	notary paper for Baden
Germany	Freiburg	Sammlung der Administrativ-Verordnungen und Bekanntmachungen für den Oberrhein-Kreis	Baden laws and regulations
Germany	Freysing/Freising	Freisinger Tagblatt	Bavaria
Germany	Freysing/Freising	Freysinger Wochenblatt	Bavaria
Germany	Fulda	Fuldaisches Intelligenz-Blatt	Hesse

Country	Published at	Title	Notes
Germany	Fulda	Kreisblatt	Hesse
Germany	Fulda	Kreisblatt des vorhinnigen Regierungsbezirkes Fulda	Hesse
Germany	Fulda	Provinzial-Blatt für das Großherzogthum Fulda	Hesse
Germany	Fulda	Wochenblatt für die Provinz Fulda	Hesse
Germany	Fürtenfeldbruck	Fürtenfeldbrucker Zeitung	Bavaria
Germany	Fürth/Fuerth	Fürther Abendzeitung	Bavaria
Germany	Fürth/Fuerth	Fürther Tagblatt	Bavaria
Germany	Fürth/Fuerth	Fürther Tagblatt/Erzähler	Bavaria
Germany	Fürth/Fuerth	Jahresbericht der Königlichen Gewerb- und Handelsschule zu Fürth	annual school report
Germany	Geilenkirchen	Gemeinnütziges Wochenblatt für Geilenkirchen und Umgegend	Rhineland
Germany	Geilenkirchen	Gemeinnütziges Wochenblatt für Geilenkirchen, Heinsberg und Umgegend	Rhineland
Germany	Germersheim	Jahresbericht über die Königliche Bayerische Lateinschule ... Germersheim	annual school report
Germany	Germersheim	Wöchentliches Unterhaltungs-Blatt für den Land-Commissariats-Bezirk Germersheim	Bavaria
Germany	Gießen	Gießener Anzeiger	500 years U Heidelberg
Germany	Görlitz/Zgorzelec	Muskauer Wochenblatt	journalism
Germany	Görlitz/Zgorzelec	Oberlausitzische Fama	Saxony

Country	Published at	Title	Notes
Germany	Gößnitz	Wochenblatt für Gößnitz und Umgebung	Thuringia
Germany	Gotha	Allgemeiner Anzeiger der Deutschen	Thuringia
Germany	Gotha	Allgemeiner Anzeiger und National-Zeitung der Deutschen	Thuringia
Germany	Gotha	Anzeiger: ein Tagblatt	Thuringia
Germany	Gotha	Gothaische gelehrte Zeitungen	scholarly
Germany	Gotha	Intelligenzblatt zur deutschen Zeitung	scholarly
Germany	Göttingen	Göttingische gelehrte Anzeigen	scholarly
Germany	Göttingen	Göttingische Zeitung von gelehrten Sachen	scholarly
Germany	Göttingen	Göttingsche Policey-Amts Nachrichten	police gazette
Germany	Grafing	Grafinger Zeitung	some limited
Germany	Greifswald	Greifswaldisches Wochen-Blatt von allerhand gelehrten und nützlichen Sachen	Pomerania
Germany	Greifswald	Intelligenzblatt von täglichen Vorkommenheiten in Pommern und Rügen	Pomerania
Germany	Greifswald	Kreis-Anzeiger für den Kresi Greifswald	Pomerania
Germany	Greiz	Fürstlich Reuß-plauisches Amts-und Verordnungsblatt	Thuringia
Germany	Greiz	Kirchlicher Gemeindeblatt für Reuss	church
Germany	Greiz	Landes-Zeitung für das Fürstenthum Reuß	Thuringia
Germany	Greiz	Sonntagsgruss unserer Heimatkirche	religious paper

Country	Published at	Title	Notes
Germany	Grevenbroich	Geschäfts- und Unterhaltungsblatt für den Kreis Grevenbroich und dessen Umgebung	Rhineland
Germany	Grevenbroich	Grevenbroicher Kreisblatt	Rhineland
Germany	Grevenbroich	Grevenbroicher Kreisblatt und landwirthschaftlicher Anzeiger für das Jülicher Land	Rhineland
Germany	Grevenbroich	Grevenbroicher Kreisblatt und Organ für die Gilbach	Rhineland
Germany	Grevesmühlen	Grevesmühlener Wochenblatt	Mecklenburg
Germany	Großenhain	Großenhainer Unterhaltungs- und Anzeigeblatt	Saxony
Germany	Grünstadt	Jahresbericht von dem Königlichen Progymnasium zu Grünstadt im Rheinkreise	annual school report
Germany	Gummersbach	Agger-Blatt	Rhineland
Germany	Gummersbach	Gummersbacher Kreisblatt	Rhineland
Germany	Günzburg	Amtsblatt für das Bezirksamt Günzburg	Bavaria
Germany	Günzburg	Jahresbericht über die Königlich Bayerische Lateinschule in Günzbug	Bavaria
Germany	Halle an der Saale	Allgemeines Journal der Uhrmacherkunst	clockmaker paper
Germany	Halle an der Saale	Der Klassenkampf	Communist party paper
Germany	Halle an der Saale	Hallisches Tageblatt	Saxony
Germany	Halle an der Saale	Hallisches Wochenblatt	Saxony
Germany	Halle an der Saale	Journal für Prediger	preacher journal

Country	Published at	Title	Notes
Germany	Hamburg	Allgemeine deutsche naturhistorische Zeitung	natural history
Germany	Hamburg	Amtsblatt der freien und Hansestadt Hamburg	Hamburg
Germany	Hamburg	Börsen-Halle: Hamburgische Abendzeitung für Handel, Schiffahrt und Politik	business paper
Germany	Hamburg	Der Spiegel	major weekly newsmagazine
Germany	Hamburg	Der treue Zions-Wächter	Jewish
Germany	Hamburg	Deutscher Beobachter oder Hanseatische privilegirte Zeitung	
Germany	Hamburg	Die rote Fahne	Communist
Germany	Hamburg	Die Zeit	news and commentary
Germany	Hamburg	Hamburger Abendblatt	
Germany	Hamburg	Hamburger Anzeiger	
Germany	Hamburg	Hamburger Börsenhalle	business paper
Germany	Hamburg	Hamburger Fremdenblatt	500 years U Heidelberg
Germany	Hamburg	Hamburger Garten- und Blumenzeitung	gardener paper
Germany	Hamburg	Hamburger Musikalische Zeitung	music paper
Germany	Hamburg	Hamburger Nachrichten	
Germany	Hamburg	Hamburger Zeitung	
Germany	Hamburg	Hamburgischer Correspondent	500 years U Heidelberg
Germany	Hamburg	Hamburgischer Correspondent (coming)	largest circulation in Europe

Country	Published at	Title	Notes
Germany	Hamburg	Hamburgisches Gesetz- und Verordnungsblatt	
Germany	Hamburg	Handlungsgehülfen-Blatt	deliveryman paper
Germany	Hamburg	Jahresberichte der Verwaltungsbehöirgen der freien Stadt Hamburg	
Germany	Hamburg	Jüdische Schulzeitung	Jewish teacher publication
Germany	Hamburg	Kritische Blätter der Börsen-Halle	stocks paper
Germany	Hamburg	Mitteilungen der Gesellschaft für jüdische Volkskunde [Alte Folge]	Jewish
Germany	Hamburg	Neue Hamburger Zeitung	
Germany	Hamburg	Norddeutsche Nachrichten	
Germany	Hamburg	Staats- und Gelehrte-Zeitung des unpartheyischen Correspondenten	Hamburg
Germany	Hamburg	Staats- und Gelehrte-Zeitung des unpartheyischen Correspondenten	
Germany	Hamburg	Staats- und Regierungsblatt für Hamburg	Hamburg
Germany	Hameln	Deister- und Weser-Zeitung	500 years U Heidelberg
Germany	Hamm	Hammsches Wochenblatt	Westphalia
Germany	Hamm	Jahresbericht des Königlichen Gymnasiums und des Realgymnasiums zu Hamm	Westphalia
Germany	Hammelburg	Jahresbericht über die königlich Bayerische Lateinschule in Hammelburg	Bavaria
Germany	Hanau	Hanauer neue europäische Zeitung	Hesse

Country	Published at	Title	Notes
Germany	Hanau	Jahresbericht über das Kurfürstliche Gymnasium zu Hanau	annual school report
Germany	Hannover	Amtsblatt für Hannover	Lower Saxony
Germany	Hannover	Der Proletarier	Communist party paper
Germany	Hannover	Hannoverscher Courier	500 years U Heidelberg
Germany	Hannover	Hannoversches Tagblatt	500 years U Heidelberg
Germany	Hannover	Jahresbericht des Lyceums 1 zu Hannover	Lower Saxony
Germany	Hannover	Notiz-Blatt des Architekten- und Ingenieur-Verein für das Königreich Hannover	architect and engineer paper
Germany	Hannover	Zeitblatt für die Angelegenheiten der Lutherischen Kirche	Lutheran paper
Germany	Haßfurt	Jahresbericht über die K. Bayer. Lateinschule zu Hassfurt	annual school report
Germany	Heidelberg	Badische Post	
Germany	Heidelberg	Der Heidelberger Student	university student paper
Germany	Heidelberg	Heidelberger Neueste Nachrichten	
Germany	Heidelberg	Heidelberger Tagblatt	dairy paper
Germany	Heidelberg	Heidelberger Zeitung	
Germany	Heidelberg	Jahresbericht über das grossh. Lyceum zu Heidelberg	annual school report
Germany	Heidelberg; Frankfurt am Main	Deutsche Zeitung	
Germany	Heiligenstadt	Eichsfelder Generalanzeiger	Lower Saxony
Germany	Heiligenstadt	Eichsfelder Tageblatt	Lower Saxony

Country	Published at	Title	Notes
Germany	Heiligenstadt	Eichsfelder Volksblätter	Lower Saxony
Germany	Heiligenstadt	Eichsfeldia	Lower Saxony
Germany	Heinsberg	Der Heinsberger Bote	Rhineland
Germany	Heinsberg	Heinsberger Kreisblatt	Rhineland
Germany	Helmstedt	Helmstedter Kreisblatt	Lower Saxony; 125 year edition
Germany	Henneberg	Henneberger Zeitung	Thuringia
Germany	Hennef	Hennefer Volkszeitung	Rhineland
Germany	Heppenheim	Verordnungs-Anzeigeblatt für den Kreis Heppenheim	Thuringia
Germany	Herford	Conivn- und Avgirte Wöchentliche Avisen	Lower Saxony
Germany	Hersbruck	Jahresbericht über die Lateinische Schule zu Hersbruck	annual school report
Germany	Hildesheim	Molkerei-Zeitung	dairy paper
Germany	Hochheim am Main	Hochheimer Stadtanzeiger	Hesse
Germany	Hof	Hofer Zeitung	Bavaria
Germany	Homburg	Jahresbericht über die Königlich Bayerische Lateinschule zu Homburg in der Pfalz	annual school report
Germany	Ingolstadt	Ingolstädter Anzeiger	Bavaria
Germany	Ingolstadt	Ingolstädter Tagblatt	Bavaria
Germany	Ingolstadt	Ingolstädter Wochen-Blatt	Bavaria
Germany	Ingolstadt	Ingolstädter Zeitung	Bavaria

Country	Published at	Title	Notes
Germany	Ingolstadt	Süddeutscher Anzeiger	Bavaria
Germany	Itzehoe	Holsteinische Stände-Zeitung	Holstein nobility
Germany	Jena	Allgemeine Literatur-Zeitung	literary
Germany	Jena	Am Wege	tourist paper
Germany	Jena	Blätter von der Saale	Thuringia
Germany	Jena	Das Volk: Thüringer Zeitung	Thuringia
Germany	Jena	Gemeinnütziges Justiz- und Polizeiblatt der Teutschen	Thuringia
Germany	Jena	Intelligenzblatt der Jenaischen allgemeinen Literatur-Zeitung	literary
Germany	Jena	ISIS, oder, Enzyclopaedische Zeitung von Oken	
Germany	Jena	Jenaer Literaturzeitung	literary
Germany	Jena	Jenaer Volksblatt	Thuringia
Germany	Jena	Jenaische Beyträge zur neuesten gelehrten Gechichte	Thuringia
Germany	Jena	Jenaische gelehrte Anzeigen	Thuringia
Germany	Jena	Jenaische gelehrte Zeitungen	scholarly
Germany	Jena	Jenaische Nachrichten von Gelehrten und andere Sachen	scholarly
Germany	Jena	Jenaische Zeitung	Thuringia
Germany	Jena	Neue jenaische allgemeine Literatur-Zeitung	Thuringia
Germany	Jena	Neuer Rheinischer Merkur	
Germany	Jena	Thüringer Kirchenblatt	religious paper

Country	Published at	Title	Notes
Germany	Jena	Thüringer Volksfreund	Thuringia
Germany	Jena	Volk	Thuringia
Germany	Jena	Volkszeitung für Sachsen-Weimar-Eisenach	Thuringia
Germany	Jena	Volkszeitung Großherzogtum Sachsen-Weimar-Eisenach	Thuringia
Germany	Jena	Weimarische Volkszeitung	Thuringia
Germany	Jülich	Jülicher Kreis-, Correspondenz und Wochenblatt	Rhineland
Germany	Kaiserslautern	Jahresbericht der K. Studienanstalt zu Kaiserslautern	annual school report
Germany	Kaiserslautern	Pfälzer Demokrat und Sonntags-Blatt	political paper
Germany	Kaiserslautern	Pfälzer Sonntagsblatt	Bavarian Palatinate
Germany	Kaiserslautern	Pfälzer Unterhaltungsblatt	cultural supplement
Germany	Kaiserslautern	Pfälzische Post	Bavarian Palatinate
Germany	Kaiserslautern	Pfälzische Volkszeitung	Bavarian Palatinate
Germany	Kaiserslautern	Pfälzisches Sonntags-Blatt	cultural supplement
Germany	Kaiserslautern	Plauderstübchen	Rhine Bavaria
Germany	Karlsruhe	Badisches Gesetz- und Verordnungsblatt	Baden laws and regulations
Germany	Karlsruhe	Gesetzes- und Verordnungsblatt für das Großherzogthum Baden	Baden laws and regulations
Germany	Karlsruhe	Großherzoglich-Badisches Regierungs-Blatt	Baden
Germany	Karlsruhe	Großherzoglich-Badisches Staats- und Regierungs-Blatt	Baden

Country	Published at	Title	Notes
Germany	Karlsruhe	Landwirthschaftliches Centralblatt	Baden agricultural paper
Germany	Karlsruhe	Landwirthschaftliches Wochenblatt für das Großherzogthum Baden	Baden agricultural paper
Germany	Karlsruhe	Notariats-Blatt für das Großherzogthum Baden	Baden
Germany	Karlsruhe	Regierungsblatt der Militär-Regierung Württemberg-Baden	Baden laws and regulations
Germany	Karlsruhe	Staats-Anzeiger für das Grossherzogtum Baden	Baden
Germany	Karlsruhe	Verordnungsblatt für die Beamten und Angestellten der Steuerverwalgung	Baden official tax paper
Germany	Kassel	Amtsblatt der königlichen Regierung zu Cassel	Hesse
Germany	Kassel	Hessische Morgenzeitung	500 years U Heidelberg
Germany	Kassel	Kasselsches Journal	extra edition
Germany	Kassel; Leipzig	Journal für Ornithologie	ornithology
Germany	Kaufbeuren	Jahresbericht über die Lateinische Schule zu Kaufbeuren	annual school report
Germany	Kempten	Allgäuer Zeitung	Bavaria
Germany	Kempten	Intelligenzblatt der königlich baierischen Stadt Kempten	Bavaria
Germany	Kempten	Intelligenzblatt des königlich baierischen Iller-Kreises	Bavaria
Germany	Kempten	Kemptner Zeitung	Bavaria
Germany	Kempten	Neueste Weltbegebenheiten	Bavaria
Germany	Kiel	Amtsblatt für das Herzogtum Holstein	Holstein
Germany	Kiel	Amtsblatt für die Herzogthümer Schleswig und Holstein	Schleswig-Holstein

Country	Published at	Title	Notes
Germany	Kiel	Landwirthschaftliches Wochenblatt für Schleswig-Holstein	Schleswig-Holstein agricultural
Germany	Kiel	Neue kielische gelehrte Zeitung	Schleswig-Holstein
Germany	Kirchheimbolanden	Jahresbericht über die Königl. Bayer. Lateinische Schule zu Kirchheimbolanden	annual school report
Germany	Kissingen/Bad Kissingen	Jahresbericht der königlichen Gewerbschule zu Kissingen	annual school report
Germany	Kissingen/Bad Kissingen	Kissinger Tagblatt	daily
Germany	Kitzingen	Jahresbericht über die Kgl. Bayerische Katholische Lateinschule zu Kitzingen	annual school report
Germany	Kleve/Cleves	Amtsblatt der königlichen Regierung zu Cleve	Rhineland
Germany	Kleve/Cleves	Öffentlicher Anzeiger der königlich preussischen Regierung zu Cleve	Rhineland
Germany	Koblenz/Coblenz	Amtsblatt der königlichen Regierung zu Coblenz	Rhineland
Germany	Koblenz/Coblenz	Coblenzer Tageblatt	Rhineland
Germany	Koblenz/Coblenz	Fest-Zeitung	gymnastics paper
Germany	Koblenz/Coblenz	Rhein- und Mosel-Bote	Rhineland
Germany	Koblenz/Coblenz	Rheinischer Merkur	Rhineland
Germany	Köln/Cologne	Allgemeines Organ für Handel und Gewerbe	business paper
Germany	Köln/Cologne	Amtsblatt für den Regierungsbezirk Köln	
Germany	Köln/Cologne	Bekleidungsgewerkschaft	clothier and hatter paper
Germany	Köln/Cologne	Der Berggeist	miner paper

Country	Published at	Title	Notes
Germany	Köln/Cologne	Der Gemeindearbeiter	community employees paper
Germany	Köln/Cologne	Der Wächter am Rhein	Rhineland
Germany	Köln/Cologne	Die Gegenwart	Rhineland
Germany	Köln/Cologne	Die Rheinische Volks-Halle	supplement
Germany	Köln/Cologne	Gewerkschaftliche Rundschau	trade union paper
Germany	Köln/Cologne	Graphische Stimme	printing worker paper
Germany	Köln/Cologne	Jahresbericht des königlichen katholischen Gymnasiums an Marzellen zu Cöln	annual school report
Germany	Köln/Cologne	Kölnische Zeitung	500 years U Heidelberg
Germany	Köln/Cologne	Niederrheinische Musik-Zeitung für Kunstfreunde und Künstler	music paper
Germany	Köln/Cologne	Rheinische Allgemeine Zeitung	Rhineland
Germany	Konstanz	Großherzoglich badisches Anzeigeblatt für den Seekreis	Baden
Germany	Kreuznach	Unterhaltungen	Rhineland
Germany	Kronach	Fränkischer Wald	Franconia
Germany	Kusel	Jahresbericht über die Lateinische Schule zu Cusel	annual school report
Germany	Kusel	Königlich-bayerisches Kreisamtsblatt der Pfalz	Bavarian Palatinate
Germany	Kusel	Neue Didaskalia	Bavarian Palatinate
Germany	Kusel	Pfälzer-Bote für das Glantal und Anzeige-Blatt für den Bezirk Kusel	cultural supplement

Country	Published at	Title	Notes
Germany	Kusel	Westricher Tagblatt	daily
Germany	Kusel	Westricher Zeitung	Bavarian Palatinate
Germany	Landau in der Pfalz	Der Eilbote	Bavarian Palatinate
Germany	Landau in der Pfalz	Der Eilbote aus dem Bezirk	Bavarian Palatinate
Germany	Landau in der Pfalz	Kreis-Anzeiger von Landau	Bavarian Palatinate
Germany	Landau in der Pfalz	Landauer Wochenblatt	Bavarian Palatinate
Germany	Landau in der Pfalz	Neues Volksblatt	Bavarian Palatinate
Germany	Landau in der Pfalz	Palatina	Bavarian Palatinate
Germany	Landsberg am Lech	Jahresbericht von der Lateinischen Stadtschule in Landsberg im Isarkreis	annual school report
Germany	Landshut	Amts-Blatt für die Gemeinden des Bezirksamts Landshut	Bavaria
Germany	Landshut	Königlich-Bayerisches Kreis-Amtsblatt für Niederbayern	Bavaria
Germany	Landshut	Kurier fur Niederbayern	Bavaria
Germany	Landshut	Landshuter Wochenblatt	Bavaria
Germany	Landshut	Landshuter Zeitung	Bavaria
Germany	Landshut	Tagblatt für Landshut und Umgegend	daily
Germany	Langensalza	Langensalzaer Kreis- und Nachrichtenblatt	Thuringia
Germany	Langensalza	Langensalzaer Kreisblatt	Thuringia
Germany	Langensalza	Langensalzaer Kreis-Wochenblatt	Thuringia

Country	Published at	Title	Notes
Germany	Langensalza	Langensalzaer Tageblatt	Thuringia
Germany	Langensalza	Langensalzaer Wochenblatt	Thuringia
Germany	Langensalza	Langensalzaisches Wochenblatt	Thuringia
Germany	Langensalza	Wochenblat für den Langensalzaer Kreis	Thuringia
Germany	Lauenburg an der Elbe	Jahresbericht	Schleswig-Holstein
Germany	Leipzig	Allgemeine Preßzeitung	press newspaper
Germany	Leipzig	Allgemeine Zeitung des Judenthums	Jewish
Germany	Leipzig	Allgemeines Repertorium der Literatur	literary
Germany	Leipzig	Allgemeiner Anzeiger für Mechanik, Optik, Elektrotechnik, Glasinstrumenten und Uhrmacherbranche	mechanical and technological
Germany	Leipzig	Ben-Chananja	Jewish
Germany	Leipzig	Blätter für literarische Unterhaltung	literary
Germany	Leipzig	Börsenblatt für den deutschen Buchhandel	bookseller paper
Germany	Leipzig	Cholera-Zeitung	cholera paper
Germany	Leipzig	Der Correspondent	printer and typesetter paper
Germany	Leipzig	Der Herold	Saxony
Germany	Leipzig	Der Jude	Jewish
Germany	Leipzig	Der Orient	Jewish
Germany	Leipzig	Deutsche Buchbinderzeitung	bookbinder paper

Country	Published at	Title	Notes
Germany	Leipzig	Die Bauhuette: Illustrierte Freimaurerzeitung	Masonic paper
Germany	Leipzig	Die Betriebsgemeinschaft der Leipziger Funkgerätebau	union paper
Germany	Leipzig	Die Grenzboten	
Germany	Leipzig	Die neue Zeit	
Germany	Leipzig	Die Uhrmacher-Woche	clockmaker paper
Germany	Leipzig	Extract der eingelauffenen Nouvellen	Saxony
Germany	Leipzig	Freimaurer-Zeitung	Masonic paper
Germany	Leipzig	Graphische Presse	lithographer paper
Germany	Leipzig	Handels-Zeitung für die gesamte Uhren-Industrie	clockmaker paper
Germany	Leipzig	Illustrirte Zeitung	
Germany	Leipzig	Jahrbuch für die Geschichte der Juden und des Judenthums	Jewish historical publication
Germany	Leipzig	Jüdisches Jahrbuch für Sachsen	Jewish Saxony publication
Germany	Leipzig	Kunstchronik	art paper
Germany	Leipzig	Leipziger Intelligenz-Blatt	Saxony
Germany	Leipzig	Leipziger Lokomotive	Saxony
Germany	Leipzig	Leipziger Mieter-Zeitung	renter paper
Germany	Leipzig	Leipziger Neueste Nachrichten	Saxony
Germany	Leipzig	Leipziger Tageblatt	daily
Germany	Leipzig	Leipziger Tageblatt und Anzeiger	500 years U Heidelberg

Country	Published at	Title	Notes
Germany	Leipzig	Leipziger Tageszeitung	daily
Germany	Leipzig	Leipziger Uhrmacher-Zeitung	clockmaker paper
Germany	Leipzig	Leipziger Völkisches-Echo	Saxony
Germany	Leipzig	Leipziger Volkszeitung	Saxony
Germany	Leipzig	Leipziger Zeitungen	Saxony
Germany	Leipzig	Leipzig's roter Straßenbahner	Socialist streetcar union paper
Germany	Leipzig	Literarisches Centralblatt für Deutschland	literary
Germany	Leipzig	Literarisches Conversationsblatt	literary
Germany	Leipzig	Mitteilungen des Gesamtarchivs der deutschen Juden	Jewish
Germany	Leipzig	Mitteilungsblatt des Ortskommittes der RGO Leipzig	
Germany	Leipzig	Musikalisches Wochenblatt	music paper
Germany	Leipzig	Neue Leipziger Zeitung	Saxony
Germany	Leipzig	Neue Rheinische Zeitung	
Germany	Leipzig	Neue Zeitungen von gelehrten Sachen	scholarly
Germany	Leipzig	Sachsenpost	
Germany	Leipzig	Sachsenzeitung	Saxony
Germany	Leipzig	Theater-Zeitung	theater paper
Germany	Leipzig	Zeitung für den deutschen Adel	nobility
Germany	Leipzig & Dresden	Illlustrirtes Familien-Journal	family paper

Country	Published at	Title	Notes
Germany	Leipzig; Berlin	Allgemeine Zeitung des Judentums	Jewish
Germany	Leipzig; Dresden	General-Gouvernements-Blatt fur Sachsen	Saxony
Germany	Leipzig-Gohlis	Freimaurer-Zeitung	Freemasonry paper
Germany	Leipzig-Wahren	Gefolgschaft Pittler	
Germany	Leisnig	Anzeiger und Amtsblatt für das königl. Gerichtsamt und den Stadtrath zu Leisnig	Saxony
Germany	Lemgo	Lippische Intelligenzblätter	Lippe
Germany	Lemgo	Lippisches Intelligenzblatt	Lippe
Germany	Lengsfeld	Der Israelit des neunzehnten Jahrhunderts	Jewish
Germany	Lindau (Bodensee)	Intelligenzblatt der Reichsstadt Lindau	Bavaria
Germany	Lindau (Bodensee)	Lindauer Tagblatt für Stadt und Land	Bavaria
Germany	Lindlar	Bergischer Agent	Rhineland
Germany	Linz am Rhein	Rheinisches Wochenblatt	Rhineland
Germany	Linz am Rhein	Rheinisches Wochenblatt für Stadt und Land	Rhineland
Germany	Linz am Rhein	Sinziger Volksfreund	Rhineland
Germany	Lippstadt	Alte Nachrichten von Lippstadt und benachbarten Gegenden	Lippe
Germany	Lippstadt	Westfälische Lehrer-Zeitung	teacher paper
Germany	Lübeck	Der Volksbote	Luebeck daily
Germany	Ludwigshafen	Berg Frei	miner paper

Country	Published at	Title	Notes
Germany	Ludwigshafen	Pfälzer Zeitung	Bavarian Palatinate
Germany	Ludwigshafen	Pfälzischer Kurier	Bavarian Palatinate
Germany	Lüneburg	Juristische Zeitung für das Königreich Hannover	judicial paper
Germany	Magdeburg	Amtsblatt der Regierung zu Magdeburg	Saxony-Anhalt
Germany	Magdeburg	Der Reichsbanner	Saxony-Anhalt
Germany	Magdeburg	Der Zeitungs-Verlag	newspaper publishers' paper
Germany	Magdeburg	General-Anzeiger	500 years U Heidelberg
Germany	Magdeburg	Hochzeits-Zeitung	Saxony-Anhalt
Germany	Magdeburg	Magdeburgische Zeitung	
Germany	Magdeburg	Volksstimme	labor paper
Germany	Mainz	Der Israelit	Jewish
Germany	Mainz	Der Katholik	Catholic
Germany	Mainz	Deutsche Weinzeitung	Rhineland wine newspaper
Germany	Mainz	Die Brennessel	humor
Germany	Mainz	Die neue Mainzer Zeitung	Rhineland
Germany	Mainz	Mainzer Eulenspiegel	humor
Germany	Mainz	Mainzer Journal	Rhineland
Germany	Mainz	Mainzer Schwewwel	humor
Germany	Mainz	Mainzer Witz-Raketen	humor

Country	Published at	Title	Notes
Germany	Mainz	Raketen	humor
Germany	Mainz	Rheinischer Humorist	humor
Germany	Mainz	Sanct-Paulinus-Blatt für das deutsche Volk	Rhineland
Germany	Mallersdorf	Mallersdorfer Anzeiger	Bavaria
Germany	Mannheim	Großherzoglich Badisches niederrheinisches Provinzialblatt	Baden
Germany	Mannheim	Mannheimer Intelligenzblatt	Baden
Germany	Marienwerder	Amtsblatt für den Regierungs-Bezirk Marienwerder	Brandenburg
Germany	Mayen	Illustrierte Sonntags-Zeitung	Rhineland
Germany	Mayen	Mayener Volkszeitung	Rhineland
Germany	Meiningen	Meininger Tageblatt	Thuringia
Germany	Memmingen	Jahresbericht der königlichen Studienschule zu Memmingen	annual school report
Germany	Memmingen	Memminger Bezirksamtsblatt	Bavaria
Germany	Mengeringhausen	Fürstlich Waldeckisches Regierungsblatt	Waldeck
Germany	Mengeringhausen	Fürstlich Waldeckisches Regierungsblätter	Waldeck
Germany	Merseburg	Amts-Blatt der königlich Preußischen Regierung zu Merseburg	Saxony
Germany	Merseburg	Amtsblatt der königlichen Regierung zu Merseburg	Saxony
Germany	Merseburg	General-Gouvernements-Blatt für das Königlich Preussische Herzogthum Sachsen	Saxony
Germany	Metten	Jahresbericht über die lateinische Schule im Benediktiner-Stifte Metten	Bavaria

Country	Published at	Title	Notes
Germany	Michelstadt	Der Odenwälder	Hesse
Germany	Miltenberg	Jahresbericht über die Königl. Bayer. Lateinschule zu Miltenberg a. M.	annual school report
Germany	Miltenberg	Miltenberger Tagblatt	Bavaria
Germany	Minden	Amtsblatt der königlich preußischen Regierung zu Minden	Westphalia
Germany	Montjoie/Monschau	Montjoiér Volksblatt	Catholic
Germany	Montjoie/Monschau	Stadt- und Landbote	Rhineland
Germany	Mülheim, Waldbröl	Waldbröler Kreisblatt	Rhineland
Germany	München/Munich	Der Nationalsozialist	National Socialist
Germany	München/Munich	Münchener Amtsblatt	Bavaria
Germany	München/Munich	Abendblatt von München	
Germany	München/Munich	Aerztliches Intelligenzblatt	physicians
Germany	München/Munich	Allerneueste Nachrichten oder Münchener Neuigkeits-Kourier	
Germany	München/Munich	Allgemeine bayrische Hopfen-Zeitung	beer paper
Germany	München/Munich	Allgemeine deutsche Fischerei-Zeitung	fishery paper
Germany	München/Munich	Allgemeine Zeitung München	
Germany	München/Munich	Allgemeiner Anzeiger für Bayern	
Germany	München/Munich	Allgemeines Intelligenzblatt für das Königreich Baiern	Bavaria
Germany	München/Munich	Amtsblatt der königlich Bayerischen General-Zoll-Administration	customs officials

Country	Published at	Title	Notes
Germany	München/Munich	Baierische Nationalzeitung	
Germany	München/Munich	Baierischer Eilbote	
Germany	München/Munich	Bayerische Israelitische Gemeindezeitung	Jewish
Germany	München/Munich	Bayerische Landeszeitung	
Germany	München/Munich	Bayerischer Kurier	
Germany	München/Munich	Bayerisches Gesetz- und Verordnungsblatt	Bavaria laws and regulations
Germany	München/Munich	Bayeristches Zentral-Polizei-Blatt	
Germany	München/Munich	Bayern-Warte und Münchener Stadtanzeiger	
Germany	München/Munich	Bayerscher Beobachter	
Germany	München/Munich	Beiblatt der Fliegenden Blätter	humor
Germany	München/Munich	Beylage zum Münchner Policey-Anzeiger	
Germany	München/Munich	Beylage zur Münchner Politische Zeitung	
Germany	München/Munich	Bürger-Zeitung	
Germany	München/Munich	Centralblatt des Landwirthschaftlichen Vereins	Bavaria agricultural paper
Germany	München/Munich	Churbaierisches Intelligenzblatt	
Germany	München/Munich	Churpfalzbaierisches Regierungsblatt	Bavaria
Germany	München/Munich	Conversernationsblatt für München und Bayern	
Germany	München/Munich	Das freie Wort	
Germany	München/Munich	Das jüdische Echo	Jewish paper

Country	Published at	Title	Notes
Germany	München/Munich	Der Bayerische Volksfreund	
Germany	München/Munich	Der Deutsche Jäger	hunting
Germany	München/Munich	Der gerade Weg	
Germany	München/Munich	Der neue Anfang	Jewish
Germany	München/Munich	Der Reichsbote	
Germany	München/Munich	Deutsche constitutionelle Zeitung	
Germany	München/Munich	Die Bewegung	student paper
Germany	München/Munich	Die Nutz- und Lust-erweckende Gesellschafft Der Vertrauten Nachbarn am Isarstrom	
Germany	München/Munich	Es muss Tag werden	
Germany	München/Munich	Fliegende Blätter	humor
Germany	München/Munich	Gesetzblatt für das Königreich Bayern	Bavaria
Germany	München/Munich	Gradaus mein deutsches Volk!	
Germany	München/Munich	Illustrierter Sonntag	
Germany	München/Munich	Intelligenzblatt des pharmaceutischen Vereins in Baiern	
Germany	München/Munich	Intelligenzblatt für das Königreich Bayern	
Germany	München/Munich	Jugend	
Germany	München/Munich	KAIN	
Germany	München/Munich	Kaiserlich und kurpfalzbairische privilegirte allgemeine Zeitung	

Country	Published at	Title	Notes
Germany	München/Munich	Königlich Baierische Staats-Zeitung von München	
Germany	München/Munich	Königlich Bayerischer Polizey-Anzeiger für München	
Germany	München/Munich	Königlich Bayerisches Intelligenzblatt für den Isar-Kreis	
Germany	München/Munich	Königlich Bayerisches Kreis-Amtsblatt für Oberbayern	
Germany	München/Munich	Kurfürstlich gnäigst priviligirte Münchner Zeitung	
Germany	München/Munich	Münchener Conversations-Blatt	
Germany	München/Munich	Münchener Guckkasten	
Germany	München/Munich	Münchener Herold	
Germany	München/Munich	Münchener Omnibus	
Germany	München/Munich	Münchener Post	
Germany	München/Munich	Münchener Ratsch-Kathl	
Germany	München/Munich	Münchener Stadtanzeiger und Münchener Ratsch-Kathl	
Germany	München/Munich	Münchener Wochenblatt für das katholische Volk	Catholic
Germany	München/Munich	Münchener Zeitung	supplement
Germany	München/Munich	Münchner Intelligenzblatt	
Germany	München/Munich	Münchner Staats-, gelehrte und vermischte Nachrichten	
Germany	München/Munich	Münchner Zeitung	
Germany	München/Munich	Neuer Bayerischer Kurier für Stadt und Land	
Germany	München/Munich	Neues Münchener Tagblatt	

Country	Published at	Title	Notes
Germany	München/Munich	Neues Tagblatt für München und Bayern	
Germany	München/Munich	Octoberfest-Zeitung	Octoberfest paper
Germany	München/Munich	Ordinari-Münchner-Zeitungen	
Germany	München/Munich	Politischer Gevattersmann	
Germany	München/Munich	Regierungs- und Gesetzblatt für das Königreich Bayern	Bavaria
Germany	München/Munich	Regierungs- und Gesetzblatt für das Königreich Bayern	Bavaria parliament paper
Germany	München/Munich	Regierungs- und Intelligenzblatt für das Herzogtum Coburg	
Germany	München/Munich	Regierungsblatt für das Königreich Bayern	Bavaria
Germany	München/Munich	Schneider-Zeitung	tailor paper
Germany	München/Munich	Simplicissimus	satire
Germany	München/Munich	Staats- und Regierungsblatt für Baiern	Bavaria
Germany	München/Munich	Süddeutscher Anzeiger	
Germany	München/Munich	Tags-Blatt für München	
Germany	München/Munich	Verordnungs- und Anzeigeblatt der königl. Bayerischern Verkehrs-Anstalten	transportation paper
Germany	München/Munich	Verordnungs- und Anzeigeblatt für die königlich Bayerischen Posten	postal paper
Germany	München/Munich	Vorwärts	
Germany	München/Munich	Wochenblatt des Landwirtschartlichen Vereins in Bayern	Bavaria agricultural paper
Germany	München/Munich	Zeitung für Feuerlöschwesen	fireman paper

Country	Published at	Title	Notes
Germany	Münnerstadt	Jahresbericht über die Königliche Studien-Anstalt in Münnerstadt	Bavaria
Germany	Münster	Münsterische Universitäts-Zeitung	university
Germany	Münster	Münsterisches gemeinnütziges Wochenblatt	Westphalia
Germany	Münster/Muenster	Allgemeines Anzeigeblatt	Westphalia
Germany	Münster/Muenster	Amtsblatt der königlich preußischen Regierung zu Münster	Westphalia
Germany	Münster/Muenster	Amtsblatt der westfälischen Wilhelms-Universität Münster	university
Germany	Münster/Muenster	Münsterisches Intelligenzblatt	Westphalia
Germany	Nassau	Herzoglich nassauisches allgemeines Intelligenzblatt	Nassau
Germany	Nauen	Osthavelländisches Kreisblatt	Brandenburg
Germany	Naumburg	Naumburger Briefe	Saxony-Anhalt
Germany	Naumburg	Naumburger Kreisblatt	Saxony-Anhalt
Germany	Naumburg	Naumburger Tageblatt	Saxony-Anhalt; to 1933 planned
Germany	Neuburg	Neuburger Wochenblatt	Bavaria
Germany	Neuburg	Pfalz-Neuburgische Provinzialblätter	Bavaria
Germany	Neustadt an der Haardt	Jahresbericht von der lateinischen Vorbereitungsschule in Neustadt a. d. Haardt	annual school report
Germany	Neustadt an der Orla	Neustädter Kreisbote	Thuringia
Germany	Neustadt an der Weinstraße	Neustädter Kreisblatt	Bavarian Palatinate

89

Country	Published at	Title	Notes
Germany	Neustadt an der Weinstraße	Unterhaltungsblatt der Neustadter Zeitung	cultural supplement
Germany	Neustadt bei Coburg	Provinzialblatt	Bavaria
Germany	Neustrelitz	Neustrelitzer Zeitung	500 years U Heidelberg
Germany	Neuwied	Der Erzähler	Rhineland
Germany	Neuwied	Der unpartheyische Correspondent am Rhein	Rhineland
Germany	Neuwied	Flugblatt	Rhineland
Germany	Neuwied	Freymaurer-Zeitung	Freemasonry paper
Germany	Neuwied	Neuwieder Intelligenz- und Kreis-Blatt	Rhineland
Germany	Neuwied	Neuwiedische Nachrichten	Rhineland
Germany	Nördlingen	Amtsblatt für das Bezirksamt Nördlingen	
Germany	Nördlingen	Bienen-Zeitung	beekeeper paper
Germany	Nördlingen	Der Hausfreund	
Germany	Nördlingen	Freimunds Kirchlidh-Politisches Wochenblatt für Stadt und Land	religious paper
Germany	Nördlingen	Intelligenzblatt der Königlich bayerischen Stadt Nördlingen	Bavaria
Germany	Nördlingen	Jahresbericht über die Königliche lateinschule zu Nördlingen	annual school report
Germany	Nördlingen	Nördlinger Wochenblatt	weekly
Germany	Nördlingen	Nördlingisches Intelligenz- und Wochenblatt	weekly

Country	Published at	Title	Notes
Germany	Nördlingen	Nördlingsche wöchentliche Nachrichten	weekly
Germany	Nördlingen	Sonntagsblatt	Bavaria
Germany	Nördlingen	Wochenblatt der Stadt Nördlingen	weekly
Germany	Nürnberg/Nuremberg	Allgemeine Handlungs-Zeitung	business paper
Germany	Nürnberg/Nuremberg	Allgemeines Intelligenzblatt der Stadt Nürnberg	Bavaria
Germany	Nürnberg/Nuremberg	Aviso oder Zeitung das ist Kurtze jedoch außfürliche Relation	Bavaria
Germany	Nürnberg/Nuremberg	Bayerischer Generalanzeiger	Bavaria
Germany	Nürnberg/Nuremberg	Bayerisches Brauer-Journal	brewers
Germany	Nürnberg/Nuremberg	Blätter für das Volk zunächst in Bayern	Bavaria
Germany	Nürnberg/Nuremberg	Der deutsche Volksbote	Bavaria
Germany	Nürnberg/Nuremberg	Der freie Staatsbürger	Bavaria
Germany	Nürnberg/Nuremberg	Der Friedens- und Kriegs-Kurier	Bavaria
Germany	Nürnberg/Nuremberg	Der Korrespondent von und für Deutschland	Bavaria
Germany	Nürnberg/Nuremberg	Der Stürmer	National Socialist
Germany	Nürnberg/Nuremberg	Die Nürnberger Estaffette	Bavaria
Germany	Nürnberg/Nuremberg	Fränkischer Kurier	Bavaria
Germany	Nürnberg/Nuremberg	Fürther Tagblatt	Bavaria
Germany	Nürnberg/Nuremberg	General-Anzeiger für Deutschland	
Germany	Nürnberg/Nuremberg	Neue Nürnbergische gelehrte Zeitung	Bavaria

Country	Published at	Title	Notes
Germany	Nürnberg/Nuremberg	Nürnberger Abendblatt	daily
Germany	Nürnberg/Nuremberg	Nürnberger Stadtzeitung	Bavaria
Germany	Nürnberg/Nuremberg	Nürnberger Tagblatt	daily
Germany	Nürnberg/Nuremberg	Süddeutsche Blätter für Leben, Wissenschaft und Kunst	cultural paper
Germany	Nürnberg/Nuremberg	Theatralisches Wochenblatt	teacher paper
Germany	Ober-Ingelheim	Rheinhessischer Beobachter	Hesse
Germany	Oettingen	Oettingisches Wochenblatt	Bavaria
Germany	Oettingen	Wochenblatt für das Fürstenthum Oettingen-Spielberg	Bavaria
Germany	Oettingen	Wochenblatt für das Fürstenthum Oettingen-Spielberg und die Umgebung	Bavaria
Germany	Oettingen	Wochen-Blatt für die Stadt und den Landgerichts-Bezirk Oettingen	Bavaria
Germany	Offenbach am Main	Der Frieden	wartime paper
Germany	Offenbach am Main	Hessische Gemeindebeamten-Zeitung	Hesse
Germany	Offenbach am Main	Neuer Rheinischer Merkur	Hesse
Germany	Offenbach am Main	Offenbacher Abendblatt	Hesse political paper
Germany	Offenbach am Main	Offenbacher Zeitung	Hesse
Germany	Oldenburg	Der Oldenburgische Volksfreund	Oldenburg
Germany	Oldenburg	Mittheilungen aus Oldenburg	Oldenburg
Germany	Osnabrück	Osnabrücker Zeitung	Lower Saxony

Country	Published at	Title	Notes
Germany	Ottobeuren	Grönenbacher Wochenblatt	Bavaria
Germany	Paderborn	Paderbornschezirks Intelligenzblatt für den Appellationsgerichts-Bezirk	Westphalia
Germany	Parchim	Mecklenburgische gemeinnützige Blätter	Mecklenburg
Germany	Passau	Der Obstbaum-Freund	orchardists
Germany	Passau	Donau-Zeitung	Bavaria
Germany	Passau	Königlich bayerisches Intelligenzblatt für Niederbayern	Bavaria
Germany	Passau	Kourier an der Donau: Zeitung für Niederbayern	Bavaria
Germany	Passau	Passauer Neue Presse	Bavaria
Germany	Passau	Passauer Tagblatt	daily
Germany	Passau	Passavia	Bavaria
Germany	Pfarrkirchen	Der Rotthaler Bote	Bavaria
Germany	Pirmasens	Sickinger Bote	Bavarian Palatinate
Germany	Plauen	Vogtländischer Anzeiger und Tageblatt	500 years U Heidelberg
Germany	Potsdam	Amtsblatt der churmärkischen Regierung	Brandenburg
Germany	Potsdam	Amtsblatt der Königlichen Regierung zu Potsdam und der Stadt Berlin	Brandenburg
Germany	Potsdam	Jahresbericht über die höhere Knaben-Schule	annual school report
Germany	Prenzlau	Jahresbericht über das Gymnasium zu Prenzlau	annual school report
Germany	Ratzeburg	Wöchentliche Anzeigen für das Fürstenthum Ratzeburg	Mecklenburg

Country	Published at	Title	Notes
Germany	Regensburg	Flora	botanical paper
Germany	Regensburg	Königlich bairisches Intelligenzblatt für den Regen-Kreis	Bavaria
Germany	Regensburg	Koniglich Bayerisches Kreis-Amts-Blatt der Oberpfalz und von Regensburg	Bavaria
Germany	Regensburg	Kreisblatt-Repertorium der Oberpfalz und von Regensburg	Bavaria
Germany	Regensburg	Mittelbayerische Zeitung	post-WW II
Germany	Regensburg	Regensburger Anzeiger	Bavaria
Germany	Regensburg	Regensburger Conversations-Blatt	Bavaria
Germany	Regensburg	Regensburger Intelligenzblatt	Bavaria
Germany	Regensburg	Regensburger Morgenblatt	daily
Germany	Regensburg	Regensburger Neueste Nachrichten	Bavaria
Germany	Regensburg	Regensburger Wochenblatt	weekly
Germany	Regensburg	Regensburger Zeitung	Bavaria
Germany	Regensburg	Gründliche Warhafftige Newe Zeitung	Calendar change 10 days
Germany	Regensburg, Hamburg	Deutsche Israelitische Zeitung	Jewish
Germany	Rendsburg	Rendsburger Tagespost	Schleswig-Holstein
Germany	Rendsburg	Schleswig-Holsteinische Tageszeitung	Schleswig-Holstein
Germany	Rheda	Gemeinnütziges Hausarchiv	Westphalia
Germany	Rheinbach	Rheinbacher Anzeige	Rhineland
Germany	Rheinbach	Rheinbacher Kreisblatt	Rhineland

Country	Published at	Title	Notes
Germany	Rheine	Jahresbericht über das Gymnasium Dionysianum zu Rheine	annual school report
Germany	Rheinsberg	HJ im Vormarsch	Hitler youth paper
Germany	Rheinsberg	Rheinsberger Zeitung	Brandenburg
Germany	Rheinsberg	Rheinsberger Zeitung: Illustrirte Unterhaltungsbeilage	supplement
Germany	Rheinsberg	Unterhaltung, Wissen und Heimat	Brandenburg
Germany	Ried	Rieder Intelligenzblatt	Bavaria
Germany	Rinteln	Jahresbericht über das Königliche Gymnasium zu Rinteln	annual school report
Germany	Rosenheim	Rosenheimer Anzeiger	Bavaria
Germany	Rosenheim	Rosenheimer Tagblatt Wendelstein	Bavaria
Germany	Rosenheim	Rosenheimer Wochenblatt	Bavaria
Germany	Rostock	Etwas von gelehrten Rostockschen Sachen	Pomerania
Germany	Rostock	Neue wöchentliche Rostock'sche Nachrichten und Anzeigen	Pomerania
Germany	Rostock	Officielle Beilage für amtliche Bekanntmachungen	Pomerania
Germany	Rostock	Rostocker Zeitung	500 years U Heidelberg
Germany	Rothenburg ob der Tauber	Amts- und Anzeigenblatt für die Stadt und das königl. Bezirksamt Rothenburg	Bavaria
Germany	Rothenburg ob der Tauber	Fränkischer Anzeiger	Bavaria
Germany	Rothenburg ob der Tauber	Jahresbericht über das Königliche Progymnasium zu Rothenburg	Bavaria

Country	Published at	Title	Notes
Germany	Rudolstadt	Allgemeine Auswanderungs-Zeitung	emigration paper
Germany	Rudolstadt	Schwarzburger Bote	Thuringia
Germany	Saarbrücken	Amtsblatt des Saarlandes	Saarland
Germany	Saarbrücken	Jahresbericht über das Königliche Gymnasium und die Vorschule zu Saarbrücken	annual school report
Germany	Sangerhausen	Sangerhäuser Kreisblatt	Saxony-Anhalt
Germany	Schewinfurt	Schweinfurter Tagblatt	Bavaria
Germany	Schleiden	Unterhaltungs- und Anzeigerblatt für den Kreis Schleiden	Rhineland
Germany	Schleiz	Jahresbericht über das Schuljahr von Ostern 1878–Ostern 1879	Thuringia
Germany	Schleswig	Amtsblatt der preussischen Regierung zu Schleswig	Schleswig-Holstein
Germany	Schleswig	Amtsblatt für die Verhandlungen der Provinzialstände des Herzogthums Schleswig	Schleswig-Holstein
Germany	Schleswig	Schleswig-Holsteinische Blätter	Schleswig-Holstein
Germany	Schnepfenthal	Der Bote aus Thüringen	Thuringia
Germany	Schrobenhausen	Wochenblatt für die königlich bayerischen Landgerichtsbezirke Pfaffenhofen und Schrobenhausen	Bavaria
Germany	Schwabach	Jahresbericht für die Landwirthschafts- und Gewerbsschule zu Schwabach	annual school report
Germany	Schwandorf	Der Naabthal-Bote	Bavaria
Germany	Schwedt an der Oder	Schwedter Tageblatt	Brandenburg

Country	Published at	Title	Notes
Germany	Schweinfurt	Jahresbericht der Königlichen Landwirthschafts- und Gewerbsschule zu Schweinfurt	annual school report
Germany	Schweinfurt	Schweinfurter Tagblatt	Bavaria
Germany	Schwerin	Der Wächter: Polizeiblatt für Mecklenburg	Mecklenburg
Germany	Schwerin	Herzoglich Mecklenburg-Schwerinisches officieles Wochenblatt	Mecklenburg
Germany	Schwerin	Mecklenburgische Anzeigen	500 years U Heidelberg
Germany	Schwerin	Regierungsblatt für Mecklenburg	Mecklenburg
Germany	Schwerin	Regierungsblatt für Mecklenburg-Schwerin Amtliche Beilage	Mecklenburg
Germany	Seelow	Seelower Tageblatt	Brandenburg wartime paper
Germany	Seesen am Harz, Goslar	Jahresberichte der Jacobson-Schule	Jewish/Christian school report
Germany	Siegburg	Anzeiger des Siegkreises	Rhineland
Germany	Siegburg	Siegburger Kreisblatt	Rhineland
Germany	Siegen	Jahresbericht der Realschule erster Ordnung zu Siegen	annual school report
Germany	Sigmaringen	Amtsblatt der preußischen Regierung zu Sigmaringen	Hohenzollern Prussia
Germany	Sigmaringen	Wochenblatt für das Fürstenthum Sigmaringen	Hohenzollern Prussia
Germany	Simmern	Der Hunsrücken	Rhineland
Germany	Simmern	Hunsrücker Erzähler	Rhineland
Germany	Simmern	Intelligenz-Blatt für den Kreis Simmen	Rhineland
Germany	Simmern	Intelligenz-Blatt für den Kreis Simmen und dessen Umge	Rhineland

Country	Published at	Title	Notes
Germany	Sobernheim	Anzeiger für Sobernheim und Umgegend	Rhineland
Germany	Sobernheim	Sobernheim-Kirner Intelligenz-Blatt	Rhineland
Germany	Solingen	Bergisches Volks-Blatt	Rhineland
Germany	Solingen	Solinger Kreis-Intelligenzblatt	Rhineland
Germany	Sondershausen	Jahresbericht über das Schwarzburgische Gymnasium zu Sondershausen	annual school report
Germany	Spandau	Spandauer Zeitung	Brandenburg
Germany	Speyer	Allgemeiner Anzeiger für die Pfalz	Bavarian Palatinate
Germany	Speyer	Amts- und Intelligenzblatt der Königlich-bayerischen Regierung des Rheinkreises	Bavarian Palatinate
Germany	Speyer	Amtsblatt der Königlich-Baierischen Regierung des Rheinkreises	Bavarian Palatinate
Germany	Speyer	Amtsblatt für das Königlich-Baierische Gebiet auf dem linken Rheinufer	Bavarian Palatinate
Germany	Speyer	Anzeige der Beamten und Angestellte im Staats- und Communal-Dienste des Rheinkreises	list of officials
Germany	Speyer	Beilage zum Amts- und Intelligenz-Blatte des Rheinkreises	Bavarian Palatinate
Germany	Speyer	Der Rheinbayer	Bavarian Palatinate
Germany	Speyer	Die Rheinpfalz	Bavarian Palatinate
Germany	Speyer	Feuilleton zum Pfälzischer Kurier	cultural supplement
Germany	Speyer	Intelligenz-Blatt des Rheinkreises	Bavarian Palatinate

Country	Published at	Title	Notes
Germany	Speyer	Jahresbericht über das Gymnasium und die Lateinische Schule zu Speyer	musical paper
Germany	Speyer	Königlich bayerisches Amts- und Intelligenzblatt für die Pfalz	Bavarian Palatinate
Germany	Speyer	Königlich-Bayerisches Kreis-Amtsblatt der Pfalz	Bavarian Palatinate
Germany	Speyer	Musikalische Real-Zeitung	musical paper
Germany	Speyer	Neue Speyerer Zeitung	Bavarian Palatinate
Germany	Speyer	Pfälzischer Kurier	Bavarian Palatinate
Germany	Speyer	Pfälzischer Zeitung	Bavarian Palatinate
Germany	Speyer	Speyerer Tagblatt	Bavarian Palatinate
Germany	Speyer	Speyerer wöchentliches Anzeige-Blatt	Bavarian Palatinate
Germany	St. Goar	St. Goarer Kreisblatt	Rhineland
Germany	Stargard	Amtsblatt der Königlichen Regierung von Pommern	Pomerania
Germany	Stralsund	Amtsblatt der preußischen Regierung zu Stralsund	Pomerania
Germany	Stralsund	Sundine	Pomerania
Germany	Straubing	Jahresbericht über die königliche Gewerbschule zu Straubing	annual school report
Germany	Straubing	Straubinger Tagblatt	Bavaria
Germany	Strelitz	Großherzoglich Mecklenburgisch-Strelitzer officieler Anzeiter für Gesetzgebung und Staatsverwaltung	Mecklenburg
Germany	Stuttgart	Allgemeine Familien-Zeitung	family paper
Germany	Stuttgart	Allgemeiner Anzeiger für Buchbindereien	bookbinding paper

Country	Published at	Title	Notes
Germany	Stuttgart	Deutsches Kunstblatt	art
Germany	Stuttgart	Die Kommunistin	Communist women
Germany	Stuttgart	Die Sonntags-Zeitung	Württemberg
Germany	Stuttgart	Eisenbahn-Zeitung	railroad paper
Germany	Stuttgart	Illustrierte Garten-Zeitung	gardener paper
Germany	Stuttgart	Illustriertes Sonntags-Blatt	supplement for East Africa
Germany	Stuttgart	Literaturblatt des Deutschen Kunstblattes	art literature
Germany	Stuttgart	Metallarbeiter Jugend	metal worker paper
Germany	Stuttgart	Neckar-Zeitung	Württemberg
Germany	Stuttgart	Regierungsblatt für das Königreich Württemberg	Württemberg
Germany	Stuttgart	Regierungsblatt für Württemberg	Württemberg
Germany	Stuttgart	Schwäbischer Merkur	Württemberg
Germany	Stuttgart	Wochenblatt für Land- und Hauswirthschaft, Gewerbe und Handel	agricultural and trade paper
Germany	Stuttgart; Augsburg	Allgemeine Zeitung	Württemberg
Germany	Stuttgart; Berlin	Buchbinder-Zeitung	bookbinding paper
Germany	Stuttgart; Tübingen	Morgenblatt für gebildete Stände	art
Germany	Suhl	Suhler Zeitung	Thuringia
Germany	Sulzbach	Sulzbacher Wochenblatt	Bavaria

Country	Published at	Title	Notes
Germany	Sulzbach	Wochenblatt der Stadt Sulzbach	Bavaria
Germany	Teltow	Teltower Kreisblatt	Prussian official press
Germany	Thurnau	Jahresbericht der Lateinschule zu Thurnau	annual school report
Germany	Traunstein	Jahresbericht über die königliche Gewerbschule in Traunstein	annual school report
Germany	Traunstein	Traun-Alz Bote	Bavaria
Germany	Trier	Allgemeiner Anzeiger	Rhineland
Germany	Trier	Amtsblatt der prdußischen Regierung in Trier	Rhineland
Germany	Trier	Der Beobachter an der Saar	Rhineland
Germany	Trier	Kurier von der Mosel und den belgischen und französischen Gränzen	Rhineland
Germany	Trier	Politische Zeitung im Saar-Departement	Saarland
Germany	Trier	Saar- und Mosel-Zeitung	500 years U Heidelberg
Germany	Trier	Treviris	Rhineland
Germany	Trier	Trierische Staats- und gelehrte Zeitungen	Rhineland
Germany	Trier	Trierisches Wochen-Blättgen	Rhineland
Germany	Triesdorf	Jahresbericht der Königlichen Kreisackerbauschule	Bavaria
Germany	Trostberg	Der Traunbote	Bavaria
Germany	Trostberg	Traun-Alz-Salzach Bote	Bavaria
Germany	Tübingen	Blätter für Polizei und Kultur	police paper

Country	Published at	Title	Notes
Germany	Tübingen	Der Kinderfreund	child welfare
Germany	Tübingen	Tübinger Blätter	Württemberg
Germany	Tübingen	Tübingische gelehrte Anzeigen	Württemberg
Germany	Vacha	Rhön-Zeitung	Thuringia, Hesse, Bavaria
Germany	various articles	Zeitungszeugen	historical commentary
Germany	Vetschau	Neue Vetchauer Zeitung	Brandenburg
Germany	Waldbröl	Waldbröler Kreisblatt	Rhineland
Germany	Waldeck	Fürstlich Waldeckisches Regierungsblatt, -blätter	Waldeck
Germany	Wasserburg	Anzeiger für den Bezirk Wasserburg	Bavaria
Germany	Wasserburg	Wasserburger Anzeiger	Bavaria
Germany	Wasserburg	Wasserburger Wochenblatt	Bavaria
Germany	Weilheim	Weilheimer Tagblatt für Stadt und Land	Bavaria
Germany	Weilheim	Weilheim-Werdenfelser Wochenblatt	Bavaria
Germany	Weimar	Der Neue Teutsche Merkur	Thuringia
Germany	Weimar	Großherzoglich Sachsen-Weimar-Eisenachisches Regierungs-Blatt	Thuringia
Germany	Weimar	Kirchenblatt für Sachsen-Weimar-Eisenach	Thuringia
Germany	Weimar	Kirchlicher Anzeiger für Thüringen	Thuringia
Germany	Weimar	Kirchliches Verordnungsblatt für Sachsen-Weimar-Eisenach	Thuringia

Country	Published at	Title	Notes
Germany	Weimar	Oppositions-Blatt oder Weimarische Zeitung	Thuringia
Germany	Weimar	Regierungs- und Nachrichtenblatt für Sachsen-Weimar-Eisenach	Thuringia
Germany	Weimar	Regierungsblatt für das Großherzogthum Sachsen-Weimar-Eisenach	Saxony
Germany	Weimar	Regierungs-Blatt für das Großherzogthum Sachsen-Weimar-Eisenach	Saxony
Germany	Weimar	Regierungsblatt für Sachsen-Weimar-Eisenach	Saxony
Germany	Weimar	Thüringer Kirchenblatt und Kirchlicher Anzeiger	religious paper
Germany	Weimar	Thüringer Kirchenblatt: Gesetz- und Verordnungsblatt	religious paper
Germany	Weimar	Thüringer Lehrerzeitung	teacher paper
Germany	Weimar	Thüringer Volk	Thuringia
Germany	Weimar	Wartburg Herold	Thuringia
Germany	Weimar	Weimarer Zeitung	Thuringia
Germany	Weimar	Weimarische wöchentliche Anzeigen	Thuringia
Germany	Weimar	Weimarische Zeitung	Thuringia
Germany	Weimar	Weimarisches Allerlei	Thuringia
Germany	Weimar	Weimarisches Wochenblatt	Thuringia
Germany	Weißenburg Bayern	Jahresbericht über die Königliche Realschule zu Weißenburg a. Sd.	annual school report

Country	Published at	Title	Notes
Germany	Weissensee	Blumen-Zeitung	flower paper
Germany	Weissensee	Numismatische Zeitung	coin collecctors
Germany	Wesel	Der Volksfreund	Rhineland
Germany	Wesel	Kreisblatt für den Kreis Rees	Rhineland
Germany	Wetzlar	Wetzlarer Kreis- und Amtsblatt	Hesse
Germany	Wiedenbrück	Der Bote an der Ems	Westogakua
Germany	Wiesbaden	Amtsblatt der Königlichen Regierung zu Wiesbaden	Nassau
Germany	Wiesbaden	Die Gemeinde	church paper
Germany	Wiesbaden	Intelligenzblatt für Nassau	Nassau
Germany	Wiesbaden	Rheinische Blätter	Nassau
Germany	Wiesbaden	Wiesbadener Badeblatt	Rhineland
Germany	Wiesbaden	Wiesbadener Tagblatt	daily
Germany	Wilhelmshaven	Wilhelmshavener Tageblatt	500 years U Heidelberg
Germany	Wipperfürth	Wipperfürther Kreis-Intelligenz-Blatt	Rhineland
Germany	Wittenberg	Das Wittenbergsche Wochenblatt	Saxony-Anhalt
Germany	Wittenberg	Wittenbergisches Wochenblatt	Saxony-Anhalt
Germany	Worbis	Treffurter Wochenblatt	Thuringia
Germany	Worms	Blumen-Zeitung	Rhineland
Germany	Worms	Mittelrheinische Sportzeitung	sports paper

Country	Published at	Title	Notes
Germany	Worms	Wormser Sport=Zeitung	Hesse sports paper
Germany	Worms	Wormser Tageblatt	Worms area
Germany	Worms	Wormser Zeitung	Rhineland
Germany	Wunsiedel	Jahresbericht der königlichen Bewerbschule in Wunsiedel	annual school report
Germany	Wuppertal	Täglicher Anzeiger für Berg und Mark	Rhineland
Germany	Würzburg	Der Postbote aus Franken: eine Würzburger politische Zeitung	Bavaria
Germany	Würzburg	Frankenzeitung	Bavaria
Germany	Würzburg	Fränkische Zeitung	Bavaria
Germany	Würzburg	Fränkisches Bürgerblatt	Bavaria
Germany	Würzburg	Herold des Glaubens	religious
Germany	Würzburg	Intelligenzblatt für Kunst und Literatur	literary
Germany	Würzburg	Intelligenzblatt für Unterfranken und Aschaffenburg	Bavaria
Germany	Würzburg	Neue Fränkische Zeitung	Bavaria
Germany	Würzburg	Neue Würzburger Zeitung	Bavaria
Germany	Würzburg	Teutsches Volksblatt	Bavaria
Germany	Würzburg	Würzburger Abendblatt	Bavaria
Germany	Würzburg	Würzburger Anzeiger	Bavaria
Germany	Würzburg	Würzburger Diözesanblatt	Catholic diocesan paper
Germany	Würzburg	Würzburger Intelligenzblatt	Bavaria

Country	Published at	Title	Notes
Germany	Würzburg	Würzburger Regierungsblatt	Bavaria
Germany	Würzburg	Würzburger Stadt- und Landbote	Bavaria
Germany	Würzburg	Würzburger Tagblatt	Bavaria
Germany	Zeulenroda	Sonntagsgruß: Reußisches Kirchenblatt für Stadt und Land	religious paper
Germany	Zittau	Lausizisches Wochenblatt	Saxony
Germany	Zittau	Zeitung des Landsturm-Infanterie-Bataillon Zittau	wartime field paper
Germany	Zülpich	Anzeiger und Unterhaltungsblatt für Zülpich, Lechenich und Umgegend	Rhineland
Germany	Zülpich	Zülpicher Anzeiger	Rhineland
Germany	Zweibrücken	Pfälzische Blätter	cultural paper
Germany	Zweibrücken	Polyhymnia	cultural supplement
Germany	Zweibrücken	Rheinbayerisches Volksblatt	Bavarian Palatinate
Germany	Zweibrücken	Zweibrücker Tagblatt	daily
Germany	Zweibrücken	Zweibrücker Zeitung	Bavarian Palatinate
Germany	Zweibrücken	Zweybrückische Zeitung	Bavarian Palatinate
Germany	Zweibrücken	Zweybrückisches Wochenblatt (and variants)	weekly
Germany	Zwickau	Jahresbericht des Gymnasiums zu Zwickau	annual school report
Hungary	Altenburg	Der Heideboden	
Hungary	Budapest	Abendblatt des Pester Lloyd	500 years U Heidelberg

Country	Published at	Title	Notes
Hungary	Budapest	Deutsches Bauernblatt	farm paper one issue
Hungary	Budapest	Deutsches Tageblatt	daily
Hungary	Budapest	Jahresberichte der Landes-Rabbinnerschule in Budapest	Jewish rabbinical school report
Hungary	Budapest	Neue Post	four issues
Hungary	Budapest	Neues Budapester Abendblatt	one issue
Hungary	Budapest	Pester Lloyd	
Hungary	Budapest	Pesther Tageblatt	
Hungary	Budapest	Vereinigte Ofner-Pester Zeitung	
Hungary	Budapest	Volksstimme	
Hungary	Mohács	Mohácser Wochenblatt	
Hungary	Ödenburg/Sopron	Der Proletarier	
Hungary	Ödenburg/Sopron	Oedenburger Arbeiterrat	
Hungary	Ödenburg/Sopron	Oedenburger Proletariat	
Hungary	Ödenburg/Sopron	Oedenburger Zeitung	
Hungary	Ödenburg/Sopron	Weckruf	one issue
Hungary	Szeged	Ben Chananja: Blätter für israelitisch-ungarische Angelegenheiten	Jewish
Israel; France	Jerusalem; Paris	Jüdische Welt-Rundschau	Jewish
Italy	Bozen/Bolzano	Alpenzeitung	Fascist paper

Country	Published at	Title	Notes
Italy	Bozen/Bolzano	Bozner Nachrichten	South Tirol
Italy	Bozen/Bolzano	Bozner Tagblatt	South Tirol
Italy	Bozen/Bolzano	Bozner Zeitung	South Tirol
Italy	Bozen/Bolzano	Das Bozner Kriegsblättchen	South Tirol
Italy	Bozen/Bolzano	Der Tiroler	South Tirol
Italy	Bozen/Bolzano	Dolomiten	South Tirol
Italy	Bozen/Bolzano	Rundschreiben des Präfekten von Bozen	wartime government
Italy	Bozen/Bolzano	Südtiroler Nachrichten	political paper
Italy	Bozen/Bolzano	Südtiroler Volksblatt	South Tirol
Italy	Bozen/Bolzano	Volksbote	South Tirol
Italy	Bozen/Bolzano	Volksrecht	political paper
Italy	Brixen/Bressenone	Brixener Chronik	South Tirol
Italy	Brixen/Bressenone	Der Ladiner	one issue
Italy	Brixen/Bressenone	Tiroler Volksbote	South Tirol
Italy	Bruneck/Brunico	Pustertaler Bote	South Tirol
Italy	Görz	Jahresbericht des K. K. Ober-Gymnasiums in Görz	annual school report
Italy	Kaltern/Caldaro	Überetscher Gemeindeblatt für Eppan und Kaltern	South Tirol
Italy	Mais	Maiser Wochenblatt	South Tirol
Italy	Meran/Merano	Der Burggräfler	South Tirol

108

Country	Published at	Title	Notes
Italy	Meran/Merano	Der Standpunkt	South Tirol
Italy	Meran/Merano	Meraner Zeitung	South Tirol
Italy	Meran/Merano	Südtiroler Landeszeitung	South Tirol
Italy	Sterzing/Vipiteno	Sterzinger Bezirks-Anzeiger	
Italy	Triest	Journal des österreichischen Lloyd	South Tirol
Latvia	Goldingen/Kuldīga	Anzeiger für Goldingen und Windau	
Latvia	Goldingen/Kuldīga	Goldingenscher Anzeiger	
Latvia	Mitau/Jelgava	Mitausche Zeitung	
Latvia	Pernau/Pärnu	Rigasche Zeitung	
Latvia	Riga	Livländische Gouvernements-Zeitung	
Latvia	Riga	Rigaische Rundschau	
Latvia	Riga	Rigische Novellen	
Latvia	Windau/Ventspils	Windausche Zeitung	
Liechtenstein	Vaduz	Der Umbruch	
Liechtenstein	Vaduz	Liechtensteiner Heimatdienst	
Liechtenstein	Vaduz	Liechtensteiner Landeszeitung	
Liechtenstein	Vaduz	Liechtensteiner Nachrichten	
Liechtenstein	Vaduz	Liechtensteiner Vaterland	
Liechtenstein	Vaduz	Liechtensteiner Volkblatt	

Country	Published at	Title	Notes
Liechtenstein	Vaduz	Liechtensteiniche Wochenzeitung	
Liechtenstein	Vaduz	Oberrheinische Nachrichten	
Luxembourg	Luxemburg	A–Z: Luxemburger Illutrierte Wochenschrift	
Luxembourg	Luxemburg	Das Luxemburger Land	multilingual
Luxembourg	Luxemburg	Das Vaterland	
Luxembourg	Luxemburg	Luxemburger Illustrierte	
Luxembourg	Luxemburg	Luxemburger Wochenblatt	
Luxembourg	Luxemburg	Luxemburger Wort	
Mexico	Mexiko/Mexico City	Deutsche Zeitung von Mexiko	
Montenegro	Cetinje	Cetinjer Zeitung	WW I paper
Morocco	Tanger/Tangier	Deutsche Marokko-Zeitung	
Namibia	Lüderitz	Lüderitzbuchter Zeitung	was German Southwest Africa
Netherlands	Amsterdam	ITF	transport workers paper
Norway	Oslo	Lappland-Kurier	Posen/Poznań
Poland	Adelnau/Odolandów	Kreis-Blatt für den Kreis Adelnau	Posen/Poznań
Poland	Beuthen/Bytom	Oberschlesische Zeitung	Upper Silesia
Poland	Beuthen/Bytom	Oberschlesisches Wochenblatt	Upper Silesia
Poland	Bialystok	Bialystoker Zeitung	

Country	Published at	Title	Notes
Poland	Braunsberg/Braniewo	Ermländische Zeitung	
Poland	Braunsberg/Braniewo	Jahresbericht über das Königlich Katholische Gymnasium zu Braunsberg	school report
Poland	Breslau/Wrocław	Amtsblatt der Königlichen Regierung zu Breslau	Lower Silesia
Poland	Breslau/Wrocław	Breslauer Zeitung	500 years U Heidelberg
Poland	Breslau/Wrocław	Breslauer Zeitung	Lower Silesia
Poland	Breslau/Wrocław	Der Breslauer Erzähler	Lower Silesia
Poland	Breslau/Wrocław	Die freie Meinung	political weekly
Poland	Breslau/Wrocław	Illustrierte Wochenbeilage der Schlesischen Zeitung	Lower Silesia
Poland	Breslau/Wrocław	Jahresberichte des jüdisch-theologischen Seminars Fraenkelische Stiftung	Jewish rabbinical school report
Poland	Breslau/Wrocław	Jüdisch-liberale Zeitung	Jewish
Poland	Breslau/Wrocław	Kunst und Volk	community theater paper
Poland	Breslau/Wrocław	Neue Breslauer Zeitung	Lower Silesia
Poland	Breslau/Wrocław	Schlesische Landarbeiter	Silesian farm worker
Poland	Breslau/Wrocław	Schlesische Priviligirte Staats-, Kriegs- und Friedens-Zeitung	Lower Silesia
Poland	Breslau/Wrocław	Schlesische Zeitung	500 years U Heidelberg
Poland	Breslau/Wrocław	Schlesische Zeitung	Lower Silesia
Poland	Breslau/Wrocław	Schlesisches Pastoralblatt	pastor publication

Country	Published at	Title	Notes
Poland	Breslau/Wrocław	Schlesisische Arbeiterzeitung	Silesia labor paper
Poland	Breslau/Wrocław	Sozialistische Arbeiter-Zeitung	labor paper
Poland	Breslau/Wrocław	Volkswacht für Schlesien	labor paper
Poland	Brieg/Brzeg	Brieger Zeitung	Silesia
Poland	Brieg/Brzeg	el	Silesia
Poland	Bromberg/Bydgoszcz	Amtsblatt der königlich preußischen Regierung zu Bromberg	Posen/Poznań
Poland	Bromberg/Bydgoszcz	Amtsblatt der königlichen Regierung zu Bromberg	Posen/Poznań
Poland	Bromberg/Bydgoszcz	Bromberger Tageblatt	500 years U Heidelberg
Poland	Bromberg/Bydgoszcz	Bromberger Wochenblatt	Posen/Poznań
Poland	Bromberg/Bydgoszcz	Oeffentlicher Anzeiger	
Poland	Danzig/Gdańsk	Amtsblatt der königlichen Regierung zu Danzig	Danzig
Poland	Danzig/Gdańsk	Danziger Dampfboot	literature, humor
Poland	Danzig/Gdańsk	Danziger Volksstimme	Danzig labor paper
Poland	Danzig/Gdańsk	Danziger Volks-Zeitung	Danzig
Poland	Danzig/Gdańsk	Danziger Zeitung	Danzig
Poland	Danzig/Gdańsk	Feldzeitung der Armee-Abteilung Scheffer	army paper WW I
Poland	Danzig/Gdańsk	Volkswacht	West Prussia labor paper
Poland	Deutsch Krone/Wałcz	Deutsch-Kroner Zeitung	500 years U Heidelberg
Poland	Elbing/Elbląg	Elbinger Anzeiger	West Prussia

Country	Published at	Title	Notes
Poland	Elbing/Elblag	Elbinger Volksblatt	West Prussia
Poland	Frankenstein/Lonsky	Frankensteiner Kreisblatt	Silesia
Poland	Frankenstein/Lonsky	Frankensteiner Wochenblatt	Silesia
Poland	Fraustadt/Wschowa	Fraustädter Kreisblatt	Posen/Poznań
Poland	Glatz/Kłodzko	Jahresbericht des Königl. Katholischen Gymnasiums zu Glatz	annual school report
Poland	Gleiwitz/Gliwice, Rybnik	Jahrbuch der k. kath. Gymnasiums zu Gleiwitz	annual school report
Poland	Gleiwitz/Gliwice, Rybnik	Rybniker Kreisblatt	Silesia
Poland	Glogau/Glogow	Der niederschlesische Anzeiger	Lower Silesia
Poland	Glogau/Glogow	Schlesische Provinzialblätter	Silesia
Poland	Gnesen/Gniezno	Kirchliches Amtsblatt für die Erzdiözesen Gnesen und Posen	Catholic bilingual
Poland	Goldap/Gołdap	Goldaper Kreisblatt	
Poland	Görlitz/Zgorzelec	Görlitzer Anzeiger	
Poland	Görlitz/Zgorzelec	Görlitzer Fama	
Poland	Greifenhagen/Gryfino	Greifenhagener Kreisblatt	Pomerania
Poland	Greifenhagen/Gryfino	Greifenhagener Kreiszeitung	Pomerania
Poland	Greifenhagen/Gryfino	Kreisblatt für die Kreisstadt Greifenhagen und Umgegend	Pomerania
Poland	Groß-Glogau/Głogów	Jahresbericht des Königlichen Katholischen Gymnasium zu Groß-Glogau	annual school report

Country	Published at	Title	Notes
Poland	Groß-Strehlitz/Strzelce Opolskie	Gross-Strehlitzer Kreisblatt	Silesia
Poland	Groß-Wartenberg/Sycow	Gross-Wartenberger Kreisblatt	Posen/Poznań
Poland	Grottkau/Grodków	Grottkauer Stadt- und Kreisblatt	Silesia
Poland	Grottkau/Grodków	Grottkauer Zeitung	Silesia
Poland	Grünberg/Zielona Góra	Grünberger Wochenblatt	Silesia
Poland	Guhrau/Góra	Guhrauer Anzeiger	Silesia
Poland	Guttenberg/Dobrodzień	Guttentager Stadtblatt	Upper Silesia
Poland	Habelschwerdt/Kladská Bystřice	Habelschwerdter Kreisblatt	Lower Silesia
Poland	Hindenburg/Zabrze	Zabrzer Kreis-Zeitung	Upper Silesia
Poland	Hindenburg/Zabrze	Zabrzer Zeitung	Upper Silesia; bilingual
Poland	Hirschberg/Jelenia Góra	Der Bote aus dem Riesen-Gebirge	Lower Silesia
Poland	Hrubieszów	Amtsblatt des K. und K. Kreiskommandos in Hrubieszów	
Poland	Kattowitz/Katowice	Kattowitzer Zeitung	Upper Silesia
Poland	Kattowitz/Katowice	Oberschlesische Morgen-Zeitung	Upper Silesia
Poland	Kattowitz/Katowice	Wochen-Post	
Poland	Kolmar/Chodziez	Kolmarer Kreisblatt	Posen/Poznań
Poland	Kolmar/Chodziez	Kolmarer Kreiszeitung	Posen/Poznań
Poland	Koschmin/Koźmiń	Amtliches Kreisblatt für den Kreis Koschmin	Posen/Poznań

Country	Published at	Title	Notes
Poland	Koschmin/Koźmiń	Amtliches Kreisblatt und Anzeiger für den Kreis und die Stadt Koschmin	Posen/Poznań
Poland	Koschmin/Koźmiń	Koschminer Zeitung und Anzeiger für die Städte Borek und Pogorzela	Posen/Poznań
Poland	Köslin/Koszalin	Amtsblatt der preußischen Regierung zu Köslin	Pomerania
Poland	Köslin/Koszalin	Amts-Blatt der preußischen Regierung zu Köslin	Pomerania
Poland	Köslin/Koszalin	Gendarmerie-Zeitung	Pomerania
Poland	Köslin/Koszalin	Kösliner Volksblatt	Pomerania
Poland	Köslin/Koszalin	Kösliner Zeitung	Pomerania
Poland	Krakau/Kraków	Krakauer Jüdische Zeitung	Jewish paper
Poland	Krakau/Kraków	Pressedienst des Generalgouvernements	wartime paper for Poland
Poland	Lähn/Wlen	Lähner Anzeiger	Silesia
Poland	Lauban/Lubań	Jahresbericht. Evangelisches Städtisches Gymnasium zu Lauban	annual school report
Poland	Laurahütte	Haus und Welt	supplement
Poland	Leobschütz/Głubczyce	Jahresbericht über das Königliche katholische Gymnasium zu Leobschütz	annual school report
Poland	Liegnitz/Lignica	Amts-Blatt der Preußischen Regierung zu Liegnitz	Silesia
Poland	Łódź/Lodz	Deutsche Post	
Poland	Łódź/Lodz	Lodzer Rundschau	

Country	Published at	Title	Notes
Poland	Łódź/Lodz	Neue Lodzer Zeitung	
Poland	Lyck/Ełk	Jahresbericht des Königlichen Gymnasiums zu Lyck	annual school report
Poland	Münsterberg/Ziębice	M	Silesia
Poland	Münsterberg/Ziębice	Münsterberger Kreisblatt	Silesia
Poland	Münsterberg/Ziębice	Münsterberger Wochenblatt	Silesia
Poland	Münsterberg/Ziębice	Stadt- und Wochenblatt	Silesia
Poland	Neisse/Nysa	Jahresbericht des Königl. kath. Gymnasiums zu Neisse	annual school report
Poland	Neustadt/Prudnik	Neustädter Kreisblatt	Upper Silesia
Poland	Neustadt/Wejherowo	Jahresbericht des städtischen Gymnasiums zu Neustadt Ob.-Schl.	annual school report
Poland	Neustadt/Wejherowo	Kreisblatt für den Neustädter Kreis	West Prussia
Poland	Neustettin/Szczecinek	Neustettiner Kreisblatt	Pomerania
Poland	Oels/Oleśnica	Lokomotive an der Oder	Silesia
Poland	Oels/Oleśnica	Intelligenzblatt für die Städte Oels, Bernstadt, Juliusburg, Hundsfeld und Festenberg	Silesia
Poland	Olkusch/Olkuß	Amtsblatt des Kreises Olkusz	
Poland	Oppeln/Opole	Amtsblatt der königlichen Regierung zu Oppeln	Upper Silesia
Poland	Oppeln/Opole	Jahresbericht des königlichen katholischen Gymnasiums zu Oppeln	Upper Silesia
Poland	Oppeln/Opole	Oppelner Nachrichten	Upper Silesia

Country	Published at	Title	Notes
Poland	Ostrowo/Ostrów	Amtsblatt des Landrats in Ostrowo	Posen/Poznań
Poland	Ostrowo/Ostrów	Kreisblatt des Kreises Ostrowo	Posen/Poznań
Poland	Pleschen/Plesczew	Pleschener Kreisblatt	Posen/Poznań
Poland	Pless/Pszczyna	Der Beobachter an der Weichsel	Silesia
Poland	Posen/Poznań	Amtliches Schul-Blatt für die Provinz Posen	Posen/Poznań
Poland	Posen/Poznań	Amtsblatt der königlichen Regierung zu Posen	Posen/Poznań
Poland	Posen/Poznań	Kreis-Blatt des Kreises Posen-Ost	Posen/Poznań
Poland	Posen/Poznań	Öffentlicher Anzeiger der königlichen Regierung zu Posen	Posen/Poznań
Poland	Posen/Poznań	Posener-Zeitung	500 years U Heidelberg
Poland	Ratibor/Racibórz	Oberschlesischer Anzeiger	Upper Silesia
Poland	Reichenbach/Dzierżoniów	Amtsblatt der königlichen preußischen Regierung zu Reichenbach	Silesia
Poland	Rummelsburg/Miastko	Rummelsburger Zeitung	Pomerania
Poland	Sandomierz	Amtsblatt des K. und K. Kreiskommandos in Sandomierz	
Poland	Schneidemühl/Piła	Amtsblatt der preußischen Regierung in Schneidemühl	Pomerania
Poland	Sorau/Żary	Jahresbericht über das Gymnasium zu Sorau	annual school report
Poland	Sorau/Żary	Sorauer Kreisblatt	
Poland	Sorau/Żary	Sorauer Tageblatt	
Poland	Sorau/Żary	Sorauer Wochenblatt für Unterhaltung, Belehrung und Ereignisse der Gegenwart	

Country	Published at	Title	Notes
Poland	Sprottau/Szprotawa	Sprottauer Wochenzeitung	Lower Silesia
Poland	Stettin/Szczecin	Amtsblatt der preußischen Regierung zu Stettin	Pomerania
Poland	Stettin/Szczecin	Entomologische Zeitung	entomology paper
Poland	Stettin/Szczecin	Greifenhagener Kreisblatt	Pomerania
Poland	Stettin/Szczecin	Jahresbericht des Entomologischen Vereins von Stettin	entomology society
Poland	Stettin/Szczecin	Ostsee-Zeitung	500 years U Heidelberg
Poland	Stettin/Szczecin	Pommersche Zeitung	Pomerania
Poland	Stettin/Szczecin	Pommersche-Zeitung	500 years U Heidelberg
Poland	Stettin/Szczecin	Stettiner Entomologische Zeitung	entomology society
Poland	Stettin/Szczecin	Stettiner General-Anzeiger	Pomerania
Poland	Stettin/Szczecin	Stettiner Zeitung	500 years U Heidelberg
Poland	Stolp/Słupsk	Stolper Neueste Nachrichten	Pomerania
Poland	Stolp/Słupsk	Stolper Wochenblatt	Pomerania
Poland	Strehlen/Strzelin	Strehlener Stadtblatt	Lower Silesia
Poland	Tarnowitz/Tarnowskie Góry	Der Bergfreund	Silesia
Poland	Teschen/Cieszyn	Amts-Blatt der k. k. Bezirkshauptmannschaft zu Teschen	Silesia
Poland	Teschen/Cieszyn	Schlesischer Merkur	Silesia
Poland	Teschen/Cieszyn	Teschner Zeitung	Silesia
Poland	Thorn/Toruń	Thorner Freiheit	

Country	Published at	Title	Notes
Poland	Thorn/Toruń	Thorner Wochenblatt	
Poland	Thorn/Toruń	Thorner Zeitung	
Poland	Waldenburg/Wałbrzych	Waldenburger Wochenblatt	Lower Silesia
Poland	Warschau/Warsaw	Warschauer Zeitung	
Poland	Wongrowitz/Wągrowiec	Jahresbericht des Königlichen Gymnasiums zu Wongrowitz	Posen; annual school report
Poland	Znin/Żnin	Zniner Zeitung	
Romania	place unknown	Siebenbürgische Zeitung	for society members only
Romania	Hermannstadt/Sibiu	Der Siebenbürger Bote	
Romania	Hermannstadt/Sibiu	Siebenbürger Bote	
Romania	Hermannstadt/Sibiu	Siebenbürgisch-Deutsches Tageblatt	
Romania	Hermannstadt/Sibiu	Siebenbürgische Provinzialblätter	
Romania	Hermannstadt/Sibiu	Siebenbürgisches Bürgerblatt	
Romania	Hermannstadt/Sibiu	Siebenbürgisches Wochenblatt	
Romania	Kronstadt/Brasov	Kronstädter Zeitung	
Romania	Kronstadt/Brasov	Siebenbürger Wochenblatt	
Romania	Temeschwar/Timosoara	Banater Deutsche Zeitung	
Russia	Gerdauen/Zhelezhnodorzhny	Gerdauener Zeitung	East Prussia
Russia	Gumbinnen/Gusev	Amtsblatt der königlichen Litthauischen Regierung	former Lithuania

119

Country	Published at	Title	Notes
Russia	Gumbinnen/Gusev	Amtsblatt der Königlichen Regierung in Gumbinnen	East Prussia
Russia	Gumbinnen/Gusev	Gumbinner Kreisblatt	East Prussia
Russia	Königsberg/Kaliningrad	Amtsblatt der königlichen preußischen Regierung zu Königsberg	East Prussia
Russia	Königsberg/Kaliningrad	Königsberger allgemeine Zeitung	East Prussia
Russia	Königsberg/Kaliningrad	Königsberger Hartungsche Zeitung	500 years U Heidelberg
Russia	Königsberg/Kaliningrad	Ostpreußische Zeitung	500 years U Heidelberg
Russia	Königsberg/Kaliningrad	Preußische Provinzial-Blätter	East Prussia
Russia	Königsberg/Kaliningrad	Preußische Zeitung	wartime paper
Russia	Moskau/Moscow	Moskauer Rundschau	
Russia	Nordenburg	Nordenburger Anzeiger	East Prussia
Russia	Ragnit/Neman	Ragniter Kreisblatt	East Prussia
Russia	Russia	Freies Deutschland	
Russia	St. Petersburg	Jahresbericht des deutschen Wohltätigkeits-Vereins St. Petersburg	German benefit society report
Russia	St. Petersburg	Neues St. Petersburgisches Journal	
Russia	Tilsit/Sovetsk	Tilsiter allgemeine Zeitung	
Russia	Tilsit/Sovetsk	Tilsiter Zeitung	
Scotland	Knockaloe	Lager-Echo	WW I POW paper

120

Country	Published at	Title	Notes
Scotland	Stobs	Stobsiade: Stobser Zeitung	WW I German POW paper
Serbia	Apatin	Die Donau	Catholic
Slovakia	Kaschau/Košice	Kaschauer Zeitung	
Slovakia	Kesmark	Die Karpathen-Post	
Slovenia	Celje	Deutsche Wacht	
Slovenia	Celje	Deutsche Zeitung	
Slovenia	Gottschee/Kočevje	Gottscheer Bote	Slovenia
Slovenia	Laibach/ Ljubljana	Laibacher Tagblatt	
Slovenia	Laibach/ Ljubljana	Laibacher Wochenblatt	
Slovenia	Laibach/ Ljubljana	Laibacher Zeitung	
Slovenia	Laibach/ Ljubljana	Landesgesetzblatt für das Herzogtum Krain	Carniola
Slovenia	Laibach/ Ljubljana	Wöchentliches Kundschaftsblatt des Herzogthums Krain	
Slovenia	Marburg an der Drau/Maribor	Marburger Zeitung	
Slovenia	Marburg an der Drau/Maribor	Südsteirische Post	
Slovenia	Pettau/Ptuj	Pettauer Zeitung	
Switzerland	Aarau	Aarauer Zeitung	
Switzerland	Aarau	Aargauer Anzeiger	Aargau

Country	Published at	Title	Notes
Switzerland	Aarau	Der Schweizer-Bote	Aargau
Switzerland	Aarau	Schweizerische Bienen-Zeitung	Aargau
Switzerland	Basel	Allgemeine Schweizerische Militär-Zeitung	Swiss military paper
Switzerland	Basel	Baseler Zeitung	
Switzerland	Basel	Basler Nachrichten	500 years U Heidelberg
Switzerland	Bern/Berne	Bernisches Freytags-Blätlein	
Switzerland	Bern/Berne	Bundesblatt	government register
Switzerland	Bern/Berne	Die Freie Zeitung	
Switzerland	Bern/Berne	Intelligenzblatt für die Stadt Bern	
Switzerland	Einsiedeln	Der Pilger	Catholic Sunday paper
Switzerland	Freiburg/Fribourg	Freiburger Nachrichten	
Switzerland	Luzern/Lucerne	Jüdisches Jahrbuch für die Schweiz	Jewish Swiss publication
Switzerland	Olten	Schweizer Schule	Swiss Catholic school weekly
Switzerland	Schaffhausen	Schaffhauser Nachrichen	paid access
Switzerland	Solothurn	Solothurnisches Wochenblatt	Canton Solothurn
Switzerland	St. Gallen	Der Erzähler	
Switzerland	St. Gallen	Der helvetische Volksfreund	
Switzerland	St. Gallen	Der Wahrheitsfreund	
Switzerland	St. Gallen	Die Ostschweiz	

Country	Published at	Title	Notes
Switzerland	St. Gallen	Neues Tagblatt aus der östlichen Schweiz	
Switzerland	St. Gallen	Schweizerische Tagblätter	
Switzerland	St. Gallen	St. Galler Volksblatt	
Switzerland	St. Gallen	St. Galler Zeitung	
Switzerland	Zürich	Amtsblatt des Kantons Zürich	Canton Zürich
Switzerland	Zürich	Der schweizerische Republikaner	
Switzerland	Zürich	Die Grüne	agricultural paper
Switzerland	Zürich	Neue Zürcher Zeitung	500 years U Heidelberg
Switzerland	Zürich	Neue Zürcher Zeitung	Swiss
Switzerland	Zürich	Sechseläuten Tagblatt	
Switzerland	Zürich	Sonnstagsblatt	
Switzerland	Zürich	Zürcherisches Wochenblatt	
Tanzania	Dar-es-Salaam	Der Ostafrikanische Pflanzer	German East Africa
Tanzania	Dar-es-Salaam, Morogoro	Amtlicher Anzeiger für Deutsch-Ostafrika	German East Africa
Tanzania	Dar-es-Salaam, Morogoro	Deutsch-Ostafrikanische Zeitung	German East Africa
Turkey	Istanbul	Türkische Post	
Ukraine	Czernovitz/Czernivtsi	Bukowinaer Post	
Ukraine	Czernovitz/Czernivtsi	Bukowinaer Rundschau	
Ukraine	Czernovitz/Czernivtsi	Czernowitzer Allgemeine Zeitung	

Country	Published at	Title	Notes
Ukraine	Lemberg/Lviv	Lemberger Allgemeiner Anzeiger	
Ukraine	Lemberg/Lviv	Lemberger Zeitung	
Ukraine	Sewastopol/Sevastopol	Deutsche Zeitung	wartime paper
USA	Allentown, PA	Der Lecha Patriot	Pennsylvania
USA	Allentown, PA	Der Lecha Patriot und Northampton Demokrat	Pennsylvania
USA	Allentown, PA	Der Liberale Beobachter und Northampton Caunty Wöchentlicher Anzeiger	Pennsylvania
USA	Baltimore, MD	Der deutsche Correspondent	Maryland
USA	Buffalo, NY	Buffalo Volksfreund	New York
USA	Buffalo, NY	Die Aurora	New York; Catholic paper; one issue digital
USA	Carlisle, PA	Freyheits-Fahne	Pennsylvania
USA	Chestnut Hill, PA	Chestnuthiller Wochenschrift	Pennsylvania
USA	Chicago, IL	Abendpost	Illinois
USA	Chicago, IL	Der deutsche Pionier	German-American biography
USA	Chicago, IL	Der Wahrheitsfreund	Mennonite paper
USA	Chicago, IL	Sonntagspost	Illinois
USA	Cincinnati, OH	Cincinnati Volksblatt	Ohio
USA	Davenport, IA	Der Demokrat	Iowa
USA	Davenport, IA	Der Tägliche Demokrat	Iowa

Country	Published at	Title	Notes
USA	Denver, CO	Colorado Post	Colorado
USA	El Reno, OK	Der Oklahoma Courier	Oklahoma
USA	Fort Scott, KS	Der deutsche Krieger	9th Wisconsin Regt. Civil War
USA	Frankfort, MD	Bartgis's Marylandische Zeitung	Maryland
USA	Frankfort, MD	Freiheitsbothe	Maryland
USA	Frederick, MD	Bartgis's Maryland Gazette	Maryland
USA	Frederick, MD	General Staatsbothe	Maryland
USA	Galveston, TX	Die Union	Texas
USA	Galveston, TX	Wochenblatt der Union	Texas
USA	Hermann, MO	Hermanner Zeitung	Missouri
USA	Indianapolis, IN	Deutsch-amerikanische Buchdrucker-Zeitung	German-American printer paper
USA	Indianapolis, IN	Indiana Tribüne	Indiana
USA	Lancaster, PA	Der Wahre Amerikaner	Pennsylvania
USA	Lancaster, PA	Deutsche Porcupin	Pennsylvania
USA	Lancaster, PA	Neue Unpartheyische Lancaster Zeitung	Pennsylvania
USA	Lebanon, PA	Lebanon Weltbothe	Pennsylvania
USA	Louisville, KY	Louisville Anzeiger	one issue; Kentucky
USA	Milwaukee, WI	Jugend-Post	youth paper

Country	Published at	Title	Notes
USA	New Berlin, PA	Der christliche Botschafter	Evangelical Association religious
USA	New Braunfels, TX	Neu Braunfelser Zeitung	Texas
USA	New Orleans, LA	New Orleanser Deutsche Zeitung	Louisiana
USA	New Ulm, MN	Der Fortschritt	Minnesota
USA	New York, NY	Aufbau	Jewish exile journal
USA	New York, NY	Israels Herold	Jewish paper
USA	Perry, OK	Neuigkeiten	Oklahoma
USA	Perry, OK	Oklahoma Neuigkeiten	Oklahoma
USA	Philadelphia, PA	Amerikanischer Beobachter	Pennsylvania
USA	Philadelphia, PA	Pennsylvanischer Staatsbote	Pennsylvania; important news
USA	Philadelphia, PA	Philadelphischer Wochenblat	Pennsylvania
USA	Philadelphia, PA	Wöchentliche Philadelphische Staatsbote	Pennsylvania
USA	Pittsburgh, PA	Berlinisches litterarisches Wochenblatt	Pennsylvania
USA	Pittsburgh, PA	Pittsburger Volksblatt	Pennsylvania
USA	Pittsburgh, PA	Volksblatt und Freiheits-Freund	Pennsylvania
USA	Reading, PA	Der Liberale Beobachter und Berks, Montgomery und Schuylkill Counties Anzeiger	Pennsylvania
USA	Reading, PA	Der Weltbothe und wahre Republikaner von Berks, Montgomery und Schuylkill Counties	Pennsylvania

Country	Published at	Title	Notes
USA	Reading, PA	Reading Adler	Pennsylvania
USA	Reading, PA	Welt-Bothe	Pennsylvania
USA	San Antonio, TX	San Antonio Zeitung	Texas
USA	San Antonio, TX	Verbands-Bote	Texas
USA	Sandusky, OH	Der Bay City Demokrat	Ohio; one issue
USA	Sandusky, OH	Der Baystadt Demokrat	Ohio; one issue
USA	Sandusky, OH	Intelligenz-Blatt	Ohio; one issue
USA	Scranton, PA	Scranton Wochenblatt	Pennsylvania
USA	St. Cloud, MN	Der Nordstern	Minnesota
USA	St. Louis, MO	Deutsch-Amerikanischer Jugendfreund	youth paper
USA	St. Louis, MO	Pastoralblatt	Catholic priest paper
USA	St. Paul, MN	Minnesota Staats-Zeitung	Minnesota
USA	Sunbury, PA	Nordwestliche Post	Pennsylvania
USA	Sunbury, PA	Northampton Republikaner	Pennsylvania
	place unknown	Appendix Relationis Historicae	
	place unknown	Newe Zeitung	
	place unknown	Newe Zeitung und eigentlicher Bericht . . .	
	place unknown	Ordinari Sontags-Zeitung, aus Deutschland, Polen Schweden . . .	

Country	Published at	Title	Notes
	place unknown	PostZeitung	
	place unknown	Resolution, Welche etliche Obristen, mit dem Fürsten von Friedland . . .	
	place unknown	Warhafftige und gründliche Zeitung	
	place unknown	Zeitung auß Wormbs	
	war theatre	Donau-Armee-Zeitung	wartime field paper

Title	Dates	Key
12 Uhr Blatt	1933–1934	ANNO
Aachener Wahrheits-Freund	1814	UDUS
Aarauer Zeitung	1819	GooBook
Aargauer Anzeiger	1840–1900 23 y; gaps	Aargau
Abendblatt des Pester Lloyd	1886 Aug	UHEID
Abendblatt von München	1830	GooBook
Abendpost	1914–1932 5 y; gaps	CRL
Abend-Zeitung	1817–1836 14 y; gaps	ANNO
Adelaider Deutsche Zeitung	1851–1862	Trove
Adenauer Kreis- und Wochenblatt	1863–1866	UBONN
Aegyptische Nachrichten	1912	ZEFYS
Aerztliche Correspondenz-Blatt für Böhmen	1873	GooBook
Aerztliches Intelligenzblatt	1858–1907 12 y; gaps	GooBook
Agger-Blatt	1845–1846	UBONN
Agramer Zeitung	1841–1912 33 y; many gaps	ANNO
Ahrweiler Kreisblatt	1861–1866	UBONN
Akademische Frauenblätter	1926–1927	ANNO
Allerneueste Nachrichten oder Münchener Neuigkeits-Kourier	1848	DigiPress

Title	Dates	Key
Allerneuestes Gradaus oder deutsches Volk	1850 Feb 15; 21	DigiPress
Allgäuer Zeitung	1852; 1864; 1866	GooBook
Allgemeine Auswanderungs-Zeitung	1846–1856	UJENA
Allgemeine Automobil-Zeitung	1900–1938	ANNO
Allgemeine Bau-Zeitung	1836–1938	ANNO
Allgemeine bayrische Hopfen-Zeitung	1861–1863	GooBook
Allgemeine deutsche Fischerei-Zeitung	1877–1908 31 y; gaps	Bio
Allgemeine deutsche Garten-Zeitung	1826–1831	Bio
Allgemeine deutsche Gärtnerzeitung	1891–1929	FES
Allgemeine deutsche naturhistorische Zeitung	1846–1857	Bio
Allgemeine Eisenbahn-Zeitung	1928–1932	ANNO
Allgemeine Familien-Zeitung	1869–1874	Ablit
Allgemeine Feuerwehr-Zeitung	1879–1879	ANNO
Allgemeine Handlungs-Zeitung	1812	GooBook
Allgemeine Kirchenzeitung	1822–1872	BavLib
Allgemeine Land- und forstwirthschaftliche Zeitung	1851–1867	ANNO
Allgemeine Literatur-Zeitung	1785–1849	GooBook
Allgemeine Literatur-Zeitung zunächst für das katholische Deutschland	1813–1816; 1865	ANNO
Allgemeine Militär-Zeitung	1826–1861	ArchOrg

Title	Dates	Key
Allgemeine musikalische Zeitung	1817–1824	ANNO
Allgemeine Österreichische Gerichts-Zeitung	1851–1918 62 y; gaps	ANNO
Allgemeine Preßzeitung	1840–1842; 1844–1845	GooBook
Allgemeine preußische Staats-Zeitung	1842	GooBook
Allgemeine Schweizerische Militär-Zeitung	1855–1906; gaps	GooBook
Allgemeine Sport-Zeitung	1880–1919; 1920–1927	ANNO
Allgemeine Uhrmacher-Zeitung	1891–1893; 1895; 1906–1907	UDRES
Allgemeine Zeitung	1810–1907 16 y; gaps	Hathi
Allgemeine Zeitung	1841; 1843	GooBook
Allgemeine Zeitung	1846–1847	GooBook
Allgemeine Zeitung des Judenthums	1851	GooBook
Allgemeine Zeitung des Judentums	1837–1922	CompMem
Allgemeine Zeitung München	1828–1870 9 y; gaps	GooBook
Allgemeiner Anzeiger	1860–1861	UBONN
Allgemeiner Anzeiger der Deutschen	1809–1828 7 y; gaps	GooBook
Allgemeiner Anzeiger für Bayern	1822	GooBook
Allgemeiner Anzeiger für Buchbindereien	1897–1907	Hathi
Allgemeiner Anzeiger für die Pfalz	1853 Apr	GooBook
Allgemeiner Anzeiger und National-Zeitung der Deutschen	1791–1849; gaps	Hathi

Title	Dates	Key
Allgemeiner Bonner Anzeiger für Industrie, Handel und Gewerbe	1859–1860	UBONN
Allgemeiner Kameral-, Oekonomie-, Forst- und Technologie-Korrespondent	1806–1807	GooBook
Allgemeines Amtsblatt	1802	GooBook
Allgemeines Anzeigeblatt	1828–1831	UMST
Allgemeines Intelligenzblatt der Stadt Nürnberg	1826–1827	GooBook
Allgemeines Intelligenzblatt für das Königreich Baiern	1819–1820	Hathi
Allgemeines Intelligenzblatt für die Fürstlich-Nassau-Weilburgischen und Nassau-Sayn-Hachenburgischen Lande	1804–1806	DiLibri
Allgemeines Journal der Uhrmacherkunst	1876–1891; 1898–1901; 1907	UDRES
Allgemeines Organ für Handel und Gewerbe	1842	UKLN
Allgemeines Reichs-Gesetz- und Regierungsblatt für das Kaiserthum Oesterreich	1849–1850; 1852	Hathi
Allgemeines Repertorium der Literatur	1819–1832	GooBook
Allgmeiner Anzeiger für Mechanik, Optik, Elektrotechnik, Glasinstrumenten und Uhrmacherbranche	1888–1889; 1895–1896	UDRES
Alpenzeitung	1926–1943	Tessmann
Alte Nachrichten von Lippstadt und benachbarten Gegenden	1787–1788	GooBook
Altonaer Nachrichten	1850–1941	Euro
Am Wege	1924–1932	FES
Amberger Tagblatt	1833 Mar	Amberg

Title	Dates	Key
Amberger Tagblatt	1864; 1869; 1872–1873	GooBook
Amberger Volkszeitung	1833 Mar	Amberg
Amerikanischer Beobachter	1808 Sep 9–1811 Aug 29	NewsBank
Amper-Bote	1877–1938 58 y; gaps	Dachau
Amtliche Linzer Zeitung	1928–1938	ANNO
Amtlicher Anzeiger für Deutsch-Ostafrika	1900–1914	Berlin
Amtliches Kreisblatt für den Kreis Koschmin	1909–1911; 1914; 1916–1918	ZEFYS
Amtliches Kreisblatt und Anzeiger für den Kreis und die Stadt Koschmin	1905; 1909	ZEFYS
Amts- und Anzeigenblatt für die Stadt und das königl. Bezirksamt Rothenburg	1866–1869	GooBook
Amts- und Intelligenzblatt der Königlich-bayerischen Regierung des Rheinkreises	1831–1837	Bavarica
Amts- und Intelligenz-Blatt von Salzburg	1818–1822; 1825; 1848	GooBook
Amtsblatt der churmärkischen Regierung	1812–1813	GooBook
Amtsblatt der deutschen Reichs-Postverwaltung	1872	GooBook
Amts-Blatt der freien Stadt Frankfurt	1857–1864	Hathi
Amtsblatt der freien und Hansestadt Hamburg	1890–1920 19 y; gaps	Hathi
Amtsblatt der großherzoglichen Oberstudiendirektion	1849–1850	UGIE
Amtsblatt der K.K.Österreichischen und K. Baierischen Gemeinschaftlichen Landes-Administrations-Kommission	1816	GooBook
Amtsblatt der königlich Bayerischen General-Zoll-Administration	1864–1880	UMUN

Title	Dates	Key
Amtsblatt der königlich preußischen Regierung zu Bromberg	1815–1851 31 y; gaps	Posen
Amtsblatt der königlich preußischen Regierung zu Bromberg	1827–1872 46 y; gaps	GooBook
Amtsblatt der königlich preußischen Regierung zu Bromberg	1883–1888	LibPol
Amts-Blatt der königlich Preußischen Regierung zu Merseburg	1816–1822; 1842; 1826–72	UMUN
Amtsblatt der königlich preußischen Regierung zu Minden	1828–1871	GooBook
Amtsblatt der königlich preußischen Regierung zu Münster	1816–1900	UMST
Amtsblatt der Königlich-Baierischen Regierung des Rheinkreises	1818–1819; 1821–1830	Bavarica
Amtsblatt der königlichen Litthauischen Regierung	1811–1816	Gumb
Amtsblatt der königlichen preußischen Regierung zu Königsberg	1814–1830 7 y; gaps	LibPol
Amtsblatt der königlichen preußischen Regierung zu Königsberg	1821–1872	UMUN
Amtsblatt der königlichen preußischen Regierung zu Reichenbach	1819	GooBook
Amtsblatt der Königlichen Regierung in Gumbinnen	1820–1873	UMUN
Amtsblatt der Königlichen Regierung von Pommern	1811	GooBook
Amtsblatt der königlichen Regierung zu Berlin	1821	GooBook
Amtsblatt der Königlichen Regierung zu Breslau	1816–1825; 1827–1872	GooBook
Amtsblatt der Königlichen Regierung zu Breslau	1821–1872 47 y; gaps	UMUN
Amtsblatt der Königlichen Regierung zu Breslau	1859; 1861; 1873; 1877; 1890	Poland
Amtsblatt der königlichen Regierung zu Bromberg	1830	GooBook
Amtsblatt der königlichen Regierung zu Cassel	1869–1872	UMUN

Title	Dates	Key
Amtsblatt der königlichen Regierung zu Cassel	1871–1908 34 y; gaps	Hathi
Amtsblatt der königlichen Regierung zu Cleve	1816–1817; 1820–1821	UMUN
Amtsblatt der königlichen Regierung zu Cleve	1816–1821	UDUS
Amtsblatt der königlichen Regierung zu Coblenz	1816–1873 54 y; gaps	UMUN
Amtsblatt der königlichen Regierung zu Danzig	1816–1903	LibPol
Amtsblatt der königlichen Regierung zu Danzig	1820–1872	UMUN
Amtsblatt der Königlichen Regierung zu Erfurt	1827–1851; 1853–1866; 1868–1872	GooBook
Amtsblatt der königlichen Regierung zu Merseburg	1834	GooBook
Amtsblatt der königlichen Regierung zu Oppeln	1816–1865 43 y; gaps	Poland
Amtsblatt der königlichen Regierung zu Oppeln	1817; 1857; 1867	GooBook
Amtsblatt der königlichen Regierung zu Oppeln	1817–1872 46 y; gaps	UMUN
Amtsblatt der königlichen Regierung zu Posen	1818; 1827	Posen
Amtsblatt der Königlichen Regierung zu Potsdam und der Stadt Berlin	1811–1872 58 y; gaps	UMUN
Amtsblatt der Königlichen Regierung zu Potsdam und der Stadt Berlin	1811–1908 86 y; gaps	GooBook
Amtsblatt der Königlichen Regierung zu Potsdam und der Stadt Berlin	1818–1908 40 y; gaps	ArchOrg
Amtsblatt der Königlichen Regierung zu Wiesbaden	1869–1871	UMUN
Amtsblatt der prdußischen Regierung in Trier	1856; 1870–1872	UMUN
Amtsblatt der preußischen Regierung in Schneidemühl	1937–1939	Pila
Amtsblatt der preußischen Regierung zu Köslin	1816–1843 41 y; gaps	GooBook

Title	Dates	Key
Amtsblatt der preußischen Regierung zu Köslin	1821–1872	UMUN
Amtsblatt der preußischen Regierung zu Köslin	1824–1867 13 y; gaps	GooBook
Amtsblatt der preußischen Regierung zu Köslin	1853–1865 10 y; gaps	Hathi
Amts-Blatt der preußischen Regierung zu Köslin	1849	GooBook
Amts-Blatt der Preußischen Regierung zu Liegnitz	1821–1872	GooBook
Amtsblatt der preussischen Regierung zu Schleswig	1869–1873	GooBook
Amtsblatt der preußischen Regierung zu Sigmaringen	1869–1872	GooBook
Amtsblatt der preußischen Regierung zu Stettin	1817–1839; 1841–1872	GooBook
Amtsblatt der preußischen Regierung zu Stettin	1817–1872	UMUN
Amtsblatt der preußischen Regierung zu Stralsund	1827–1872 39 y; gaps	GooBook
Amtsblatt der preußischen Regierung zu Stralsund	1827–1872 41 y; gaps	UMUN
Amtsblatt der Regierung zu Aachen	1845	GooBook
Amtsblatt der Regierung zu Aachen	1817–1906 48 y; gaps	Hathi
Amtsblatt der Regierung zu Aachen	1826–1906 44 y; gaps	GooBook
Amtsblatt der Regierung zu Frankfurt an der Oder	1874	Hathi
Amtsblatt der Regierung zu Frankfurt an der Oder	1816; 1818–1872	UMUN
Amtsblatt der Regierung zu Magdeburg	1823	GooBook
Amtsblatt der Regierung zu Magdeburg	1816–1836	Hathi
Amtsblatt der Regierung zu Magdeburg	1817–1873	UMUN

Title	Dates	Key
Amtsblatt der Stadt Altona	1920–1933	UHBG
Amtsblatt der westfälischen Wilhelms-Universität Münster	1938–1944	UMST
Amtsblatt des großherzoglichen Ministerium der Finanzen	1885–1914	Hathi
Amtsblatt des großherzoglichen Oberschulraths	1833–1849	UGIE
Amtsblatt des Kantons Zürich	1859–1863, 1865–1884	Hathi
Amtsblatt des Kreises Olkusz	1916	Poland
Amtsblatt des Landrats in Ostrowo	1943	Poland
Amtsblatt des preußischen Post-Departements	1867	GooBook
Amtsblatt des Saarlandes	1945–2009	UREG
Amtsblatt für das Bezirksamt Günzburg	1869–1873	GooBook
Amtsblatt für das Bezirksamt Nördlingen	1873	GooBook
Amtsblatt für das Bezirksamts und Amtsgericht Aichach	1870	Bavarica
Amtsblatt für das Herzogtum Holstein	1851–1852	UMUN
Amtsblatt für das Königlich-Baierische Gebiet auf dem linken Rheinufer	1816–1817	Bavarica
Amtsblatt für den Landesteil Birkenfeld	1858–1859; 1864	DiLibri
Amtsblatt für den Regierungs-Bezirk Arnsberg	1821–1872	UMUN
Amtsblatt für den Regierungs-Bezirk Arnsberg	1821–1872 49 y; gaps	GooBook
Amtsblatt für den Regierungsbezirk Düsseldorf	1816–1987 !	UDUS
Amtsblatt für den Regierungsbezirk Düsseldorf	1820–1866 44 y; gaps	GooBook

Title	Dates	Key
Amtsblatt für den Regierungsbezirk Köln	1827–1872	GooBook
Amtsblatt für den Regierungs-Bezirk Marienwerder	1820–1825; 1828–1869; 1871	UMUN
Amtsblatt für den Stadtkreis Frankfurt a. M.	1914–1915	UFFM
Amts-Blatt für die Gemeinden des Bezirksamts Landshut	1864; 1866–1867	GooBook
Amtsblatt für die Herzogthümer Schleswig und Holstein	1849	ZEFYS
Amtsblatt für die königlichen Bezirksämter Forchheim und Ebermannstadt	1868	Bavarica
Amtsblatt für die Provinz Westfalen	1815	Hathi
Amtsblatt für die Verhandlungen der Provinzialstände des Herzogthums Schleswig	1836	GooBook
Amtsblatt für Hannover	1867–1872	UMUN
An der schönen blauen Donau	1886–1895	ANNO
Andernacher Burger-Blatt	1837; 1855–1862	UBONN
Andreas Hofer Wochenblatt	1878–1906	Tessmann
Annalen	1787	UBONN
Ansbacher Morgenblatt	1846–1863 6 y; gaps	GooBook
Anzeige der Beamten und Angestellte im Staats- und Communal-Dienste des Rheinkreises	1827	GooBook
Anzeigeblatt der städtischen Behörden zu Frankfurt am Main	1914	UFFM
Anzeigen des Fürstenthums Schaumburg-Lippe	1850–1859	GooBook
Anzeiger des Siegkreises	1855–1862	UBONN

Title	Dates	Key
Anzeiger für den Bezirk Wasserburg	1872	GooBook
Anzeiger für die Bezirke Bludenz und Montafon	1885–1941	ANNO
Anzeiger für Goldingen und Windau	1927–1929	Latvia
Anzeiger für Sobernheim und Umgegend	1860; 1862	UBONN
Anzeiger und Amtsblatt für das königl. Gerichtsamt und den Stadtrath zu Leisnig	1859–1864	UDRES
Anzeiger und Unterhaltungsblatt für Zülpich, Lechenich und Umgegend	1857–1867	UBONN
Anzeiger: ein Tagblatt	1791–1793	UJENA
Appendix Relationis Historicae	1632	UBREM
Arbeiter Schachzeitung	1921–1922	ANNO
Arbeiterinnen-Zeitung	1892–1902; 1914–1919	ANNO
Arbeiterwille	1890–1928	ANNO
Arbeiterwohlfahrt	1926–1933	FES
Arbeiter-Zeitung	1889–1936	ANNO
Arbeiter-Zeitung	1945–1989	ArbZtg
Arbeiter-Zeitung für Schlesien und Oberschlesien	1926; 1928–1933	FES
Areler Zeitung	1918 Nov 12	Euro
Argentinisches Wochenblatt	1942–1946	ZEFYS
Armeeblatt	1914; 1916–1919	ANNO
Armee-Zeitung der 2. Armee	1914–1918	BNF

Title	Dates	Key
Arnsberger Intelligenz-Blatt	1803 Sep 27?	WikiComm
Aschaffenburger Wochenblatt	1824; 1826–1828	GooBook
Aschaffenburger Zeitung	1866–1873	GooBook
Aufbau	1951–2004	Baeck
Aufwärts	1932	DHM
Augsburger Anzeigeblatt	1861–1862; 1866; 1868	GooBook
Augsburger Neuester Nachrichten	1862–1873	GooBook
Augsburger Post-Zeitung	1840; 1854–1855; 1858	GooBook
Augsburger Sonntagsblatt	1873	GooBook
Augsburger Tagblatt	1863; 1865–1866; 1868	GooBook
Augspurgische Ordinari Postzeitung	1770–1806	Augsburg
Austria: Tagblatt für Handel und Gewerbe	1851	GooBook
Auszug aus der Tagespresse	1917–1918	ANNO
Aviso oder Zeitung das ist Kurtze jedoch außfürliche Relation	1614	UBREM
A-Z: Luxemburger Illutrierte Wochenschrift	1933–1940	Lux
Bacillus verus	1916–1918	USTR
Bade- und Reise-Journal	1876–1930 72 y; gaps	ANNO
Badener Bezirks-Blatt	1880–1896	ANNO
Badener Lazarett-Zeitung	1916–1918	UHEID

Title	Dates	Key
Badener Lazarett-Zeitung	1918?	UHEID
Badener Zeitungen	1896–1943	ANNO
Badische Post	1919; 1923	UHEID
Badisches Gesetz- und Verordnungsblatt	1803–1921 96 y; gaps	Hathi
Baierische Nationalzeitung	1808; 1810–1811; 1813–1819	GooBook
Baierischer Eilbote	1840; 1843–1848; 1850	GooBook
Bamberger Journal	1882	Hathi
Bamberger Neueste Nachrichten	1869; 1871	GooBook
Bamberger Tagblatt	1866	GooBook
Banater Deutsche Zeitung	1936–1939	DiFMOE
Bapaumer Zeitung am Mittag	1914 Nov 14	BNF
Bar Kochba	1919–1921	CompMem
Barmer Wochenblatt	1838–1859	UBONN
Barmer Zeitung	1886 Aug	UHEID
Bartgis's Maryland Gazette	1792 May 22	NewsBank
Bartgis's Marylandische Zeitung	1789 Feb 18	NewsBank
Baseler Zeitung	1831–1836	GooBook
Basler Nachrichten	1886 Aug	UHEID
Bauern-Zeitung aus Frauendorf	1826	GooBook

Title	Dates	Key
Bayerische Israelitische Gemeindezeitung	1925–1937	CompMem
Bayerische Landeszeitung	1869	GooBook
Bayerische Ostmark Coburger National-Zeitung	1939–1940	DigiPress
Bayerischer Generalanzeiger	1862	GooBook
Bayerischer Kurier	1859–1869	GooBook
Bayerisches Brauer-Journal	1891–1919	DigiPress
Bayerisches Gesetz- und Verordnungsblatt	1875–1922 39 y; gaps	Hathi
Bayerisches Gesetz- und Verordnungsblatt	1875–1923 (gaps)	Hathi
Bayeristches Zentral-Polizei-Blatt	1866–1914	Bavarica
Bayern-Warte und Münchener Stadtanzeiger	1921	DigiPress
Bayerscher Beobachter	1829	GooBook
Bayreuther Intelligenz-Zeitung	1796	GooBook
Bayreuther Zeitung	1785–1842 8 y; gaps	GooBook
Beiblatt der Fliegenden Blätter	1883–1920 (more coming)	UHEID
Beiblatt der Freisinnigen Zeitung	1886 Aug	UHEID
Beilage zum Amts- und Intelligenz-Blatte des Rheinkreises	1836	GooBook
Beilage zur politischen Chronik	1911–1918	ANNO
Beiträge zur Ausbreitung nützlicher Kenntnisse	1784–1785	UBONN
Bekleidungsgewerkschaft	1921; 1923–1933	FES

Title	Dates	Key
Belehrendes und Unterhaltendes	1895–1896; 1904–1905	ANNO
Ben-Chananja	1858–1867	CompMem
Bensberger Volkszeitung	1907–1929	UBONN
Bensberg-Gladbacher Anzeiger	1870–1907	UBONN
Berg Frei	1921–1923	FES
Berg- und Hüttenmännische Zeitung	1870–1881	GooBook
Bergische Wacht	1907–1919; 1932	UBONN
Bergischer Agent	1903–1905	UBONN
Bergischer Türmer	1905–1912	UBONN
Bergisches Volks-Blatt	1851–1867	UBONN
Bergisch-Gladbacher Volkszeitung	1906–1929	UBONN
Bergsträßer Anzeigeblatt	1920–1934 6 y; gaps	UDARM
Berichte für die Lehranstalt für die Wissenschaft des Judentums	1874–1938	CompMem
Berliner Börsen-Courier	1886 Aug	UHEID
Berliner Börsen-Zeitung	1857–1895	ZEFYS
Berliner Courier	1886 Aug	UHEID
Berliner Gerichts-Zeitung	1853–1898	ZEFYS
Berliner Krakehler	1848 May 14	MICHAEL
Berliner Morgenpost	1933	ZEFYS

143

Title	Dates	Key
Berliner Tageblatt und Handels-Zeitung	1878–1928	ZEFYS
Berliner Vereinsbote	1896–1897	CompMem
Berliner Volks-Zeitung	1919–1920	CRL
Berliner Zeitung	1945–1993 (special login)	ZEFYS
Berlinische Nachrichten von Staats- und gelehrten Sachen	1812–1814	Hathi
Berlinische privilierte Zeitung	1740	ZEFYS
Berlinisches litterarisches Wochenblatt	1776	Hathi
Berlinisches litterarisches Wochenblatt	1860–1865	GooNews
Bernisches Freytags-Blätlein	1722–1724	DiFMOE
Betriebsgemeinschaft Renner	1944	DHM
Betriebsräte-Zeitschrift des DMV	1920–1931	FES
Beylage zum Münchner Policey-Anzeiger	1824	GooBook
Beylage zur Münchner Politische Zeitung	1820	GooBook
Bialystoker Zeitung	1916–1917; 1919	Euro
Bienen-Zeitung	1860; 1883	GooBook
Bitburger Kreis- und Intelligenzblatt	1854–1867	UBONN
Blätter für das Volk zunächst in Bayern	1848	DigiPress
Blätter für literarische Unterhaltung	1826–1867	ANNO
Blätter für Polizei und Kultur	1801–1803	UBIEL

Title	Dates	Key
Blätter für religiöse Erziehung	1913–1914	UJENA
Blätter für Theater, Musik und Kunst	1855–1873	ANNO
Blätter von der Saale	1850–1858	UJENA
Blau-Weiß-Blätter	1913–1919	CompMem
Blau-Weiß-Blätter (Neue Folge)	1923–1925	CompMem
Blau-Weiß-Blätter Führerheft	1917–1923	CompMem
Blumen-Zeitung	1837–1848 6 y; gaps	Bio
Bochumer Kreisblatt	1842–1874	UMST
Bockenheimer Anzeiger	1914	UFFM
Bohemia	1846–1914	Kram
Bohemia, ein Unterhaltungsblatt	1832–1845	Kram
Bohemia, oder Unterhaltungsblätter für gebildete Stände	1830–1832	Kram
Böhmerwald Volksbote	1913–1919	ANNO
Böhmerwald-Volksbote	1915–1917	ANNO
Bonner Anzeiger	1850	UBONN
Bonner Chronik	1890–1891	UBONN
Bonner Dekadenschrift	1794–1795	UBONN
Bonner Tageblatt	1883–1890	UBONN
Bonner Volksblatt	1862	UBONN

Title	Dates	Key
Bonner Volkszeitung	1882–1906	UBONN
Bonner Wochenblatt	1816–1850	UBONN
Bonner Zeitung	1848	UBONN
Bonner Zeitung	1824–1830	UBONN
Bonner Zeitung	1851–1919	UBONN
Bönnischer Sitten, Staats- und Geschichtslehrer	1772	UBONN
Bönnisches Wochenblatt	1785–1788	UBONN
Bönnisches Wochenblatt	1814–1815	UBONN
Börsenblatt für den deutschen Buchhandel	1872	GooBook
Börsen-Halle: Hamburgische Abendzeitung für Handel, Schiffahrt und Politik	1833	GooBook
Botanische Zeitung	1844–1910	Bio
Bozner Nachrichten	1894–1925	Tessmann
Bozner Tagblatt	1943–1945	Tessmann
Bozner Zeitung	1842–1918	Tessmann
Brand Aus	1960–present	ANNO
Braunschweigische landwirtschaftliche Zeitung	1882–1899 coming	UBRAU
Bregenzer Wochenblatt	1793–1863 67 y; gaps	ANNO
Bregenzer/Vorarlberger Tagblatt	1889–1915; 1919–1943	ANNO
Bremer Zeitung	1817–1818; 1820	GooBook

Title	Dates	Key
Breslauer Zeitung	1886 Aug	UHEID
Brieger Zeitung	1914 Oct 1; 1943 Mar 16	ZEFYS
Brioni Insel-Zeitung	1910–1913	ANNO
Brixener Chronik	1888–1925	Tessmann
Bromberger Tageblatt	1886 Aug	UHEID
Bromberger Wochenblatt	1846–1861	Pol Byd
Brünner Hebammen-Zeitung	1910–1918	ANNO
Brünner Tagesbote	1851–1944	DiFMOE
Buchbinder-Zeitung	1874; 1885–1909	FES
Buckower Local-Anzeiger	1943–1944	ZEFYS
Budissener Nachrichten	1828–1868	UDRES
Buffalo Volksfreund	1891 annotated	Archivaria
Bukowinaer Post	1893–1914	ANNO
Bukowinaer Rundschau	1883–1907	ANNO
Bundesblatt	1849–1990	CH
Burgenländische Freiheit	1921–1934; 1946–2007	BF-Archiv
Bürger-Zeitung	1867–1868	GooBook
Bütower Anzeiger	1916–1918	ZEFYS
Cameralistische Zeitung	1836	GooBook

Title	Dates	Key
Carinthia	1842	AustLit
Casselische Polizey- und Commerzien-Zeitung	1735–1821	UKASL
Central- und Bezirks-Amtsblatt für Elsass-Lothringen	1883–1907 25 y; gaps	Hathi
Central-Anzeiger für jüdische Literatur	1890	CompMem
Centralblatt der Bauverwaltung	1889	GooBook
Centralblatt des Landwirthschaftlichen Vereins	1836–1840	Hathi
Central-Blatt für das deutsche Reich	1873; 1875–1876; 1878	GooBook
Central-Blatt für das deutsche Reich	1880–1918	Hathi
Central-Verein Zeitung	1922–1938	CompMem
Cetinjer Zeitung	1916–1918	ANNO
Chamlagne-Kriegs-Zeitung	1916	BNF
Champagner Kriegs-Zeitung	1917–1918; scattered	UHEID
Charlottenburger Zeitung	1880–1880	ZEFYS
Chemische Zeitung	1879; 1881	GooBook
Chestnuthiller Wochenschrift	1790 Aug 10–1793 Aug 20	NewsBank
Cholera-Zeitung	1831	GooBook
Christlich-soziale Arbeiter-Zeitung	1902–1934	ANNO
Churbaierisches Intelligenzblatt	1766–1776	BavLib
Churbaierisches Intelligenzblatt	1770; 1773	GooBook

Title	Dates	Key
Churpfalzbaierisches Regierungsblatt	1802–1805	Hathi
Cincinnati Volksblatt	1914–1918	Chron
Coblenzer Tageblatt	1863–1865	UBONN
Coburger Nationalzeitung	1930–1934; 1940–1945	DigiPress
Coburger Regierungs-Blatt	1919–1920	DigiPress
Coburger Regierungs-Blatt / Bezirksamt Coburg	1921–1922	DigiPress
Coburger Zeitung	1854–1935 74 y; gaps	BavLib
Coburgische wöchentliche Anzeige	1777–1782	Hathi
Cochemer Anzeiger	1851–1860	UBONN
Colorado Post	1874–1880	Colo
Conivn- und Avgirte Wöchentliche Avisen	1630	UBREM
Conservative Provinzial-Zeitung für Rheinland und Westphalen	1866	UBONN
Constitutionelle Zeitung	1848	Euro
Conversernationsblatt für München und Bayern	1834	GooBook
Cook's-Welt-Reise-Zeitung	1890–1891; 1894–1916	ANNO
Cur-Liste Bad Ischl	1842–1938 89 y; gaps	ANNO
Czernowitzer Allgemeine Zeitung	1904–1914; 1917–1918	ANNO
Daheim	1914–1918	UHEID
Danziger Dampfboot	1834–1852	ZEFYS

Title	Dates	Key
Danziger Volksstimme	1920–1932; 1936	FES
Danziger Volks-Zeitung	1934–1937	GDAN
Danziger Zeitung	1808–1809; 1812–1813; 1819	GDAN
Danziger Zeitung	1886 Aug	UHEID
Darmstädter Freie Presse	1887	UDARM
Darmstädter Tageblatt	1886 Aug	UHEID
Darmstädter Zeitung	1872–1920	UDARM
Das Bozner Kriegsblättchen	1796	Tessmann
Das Echo	1890; 1893	GooBook
Das Frauen-Blatt	1847–1919 22 y; gaps	ANNO
Das freie Wort	1848	DigiPress
Das illustrierte Blatt	1914	UFFM
Das Inland	1836–1863	UTART
Das jüdische Echo	1917	Hathi
Das Kleine Journal	1927	DHM
Das Luxemburger Land	1882–1886	Lux
Das neue Reich	1919; 1925; 1929–1932	DHM
Das Painier des Fortschrittes	1848 Nov 9	DHM
Das Recht der Feder	1901–1902	ZEFYS

Title	Dates	Key
Das Riesengebirge in Wort und Bild	1881–1898	DiFMOE
Das rote Berlin	1932	DHM
Das Vaterland	1854–1916	ANNO
Das Vaterland	1869–1870	Lux
Das Volk: Thüringer Zeitung	1921–1926 (more coming)	UJENA
Das Wienerblättchen	1783–1785; 1788; 1792	ANNO
Das Wittenbergsche Wochenblatt	1768–1785	ANNO
Das Wort der Frau	1932	Euro
Das Zelt	1924	CompMem
Deborah	1866	CompMem
Deggendorfer Donaubote	1871–1873	GooBook
Deister- und Weser-Zeitung	1886	UHEID
Der Adler	1838–1843	ANNO
Der Alpenfreund	1895–1896; 1921–1943	ANNO
Der Architekt	1895–1921 24 y; gaps	ANNO
Der Armierer	1917–1918	USTR
Der Bauernbündler	1906–1938	ANNO
Der Bautechniker	1880–1921	ANNO
Der Bay City Demokrat	1856	Sandusky

Title	Dates	Key
Der bayerische Landwehrmann	1914–1918	USTR
Der Bayerische Volksfreund	1826	GooBook
Der Baystadt Demokrat	1906	Sandusky
Der Beobachter an der Saar	1798–1799	DiLibri
Der Beobachter an der Weichsel	1806–1806	ZEFYS
Der Bergfreund	1839	ZEFYS
Der Berggeist	1856–1873	GooBook
Der Bote an der Ems	1867	UMST
Der Bote aus dem Riesen-Gebirge	1813–1914 7 y; gaps	Euro
Der Bote aus Thüringen	1788–1816	UJENA
Der Bote aus Thüringen	1789–1809 10 y; gaps	GooBook
Der Bote für Tirol	1813–1919	Tessmann
Der Breslauer Erzähler	1835	GooBook
Der Brummbär	1933	ZEFYS
Der Bureauangestellte	1906–1919	FES
Der Burggräfler	1883–1926	Tessmann
Der Calculator an der Elbe	1872–1844	UDRES
Der Champagne-Kamerad	1915–1918	UHEID
Der christliche Botschafter	1840–1849	Hathi

Title	Dates	Key
Der Correspondent	1863–1869; 1933	FES
Der Demokrat	1848	Euro
Der Demokrat	1862–1865	Chron
Der deutsche Correspondent	1841–1918	Chron
Der deutsche Krieger	1862	Gale
Der deutsche Pionier	1869–1887	NAUSA
Der deutsche Volksbote	1832	GooBook
Der Drahtverhau	1915–1918	UHEID
Der Eilbote	1837–1866	GooBook
Der Eilbote aus dem Bezirk	1833–1836	GooBook
Der Erzähler	1806–1865	Switz
Der Erzähler	1849–1851	UBONN
Der Fortschritt	1891–1915	Chron
Der freie Angestellte	1919–1933	FES
Der freie Staatsbürger	1848–1850	DigiPress
Der Freiheitskampf	1945	Euro
Der Freund der Wahrheit und des Volkes	1848–1849	DigiPress
Der Frieden	1914–1915	UFFM
Der Friedens- und Kriegs-Kurier	1822–1839	GooBook

Title	Dates	Key
Der Funke	1932–1933	FES
Der Gemeindearbeiter	1913–1922	FES
Der gerade Weg	1932–1933	DigiPress
Der Hausbesitzer/Hausherren Zeitung	1892–1916; 1922–1937	ANNO
Der Hausfreund	1839	GooBook
Der Hausfreund	1838–1841	Bavarica
Der Heideboden	1919 Sep 10; 17; 24	DiFMOE
Der Heidelberger Student	1929–1938	UHEID
Der Heinsberger Bote	1851–1857	UBONN
Der helvetische Volksfreund	1799–1801	Switz
Der Herold	1848 Aug 16	Lpzg
Der Horchposten des Kgl. Württembergischen Gebirgsbattaillions	1917–1918	UHEID
Der Humorist	1837–1862	ANNO
Der Hunsrücken	1839–1842	UBONN
Der Internationale Klassenkampf	1936	DHM
Der Israelit	1860–1938	CompMem
Der Israelit des neunzehnten Jahrhunderts	1840–1848	CompMem
Der israelitische Volkslehrer	1851–1860	CompMem
Der Jude	1768–1772	CompMem

Title	Dates	Key
Der Jude	1832–1833; 1835	CompMem
Der Jude	1916–1928	CompMem
Der Judenkenner	1935	DHM
Der jüdische Arbeiter	1927–1934	CompMem
Der jüdische Student	1902–1903	CompMem
Der jüdische Student (Neue Folge)	1904–1933	CompMem
Der jüdische Wille (Alte Folge)	1918–1920	CompMem
Der jüdische Wille (Neue Folge)	1933–1937	CompMem
Der junge Jude	1927–1931	CompMem
Der Kämpfer	1920 Jun 26	DHM
Der Kampfruf	1929	DHM
Der Katholik	1821–1823	UTUB
Der Kinderfreund	1778–1781	UGOT
Der Kinobesitizer	1917–1919	ANNO
Der Klassenkampf	1931 May 3	DHM
Der Korrespondent von und für Deutschland	1813	GooBook
Der Kroatische Korrespondent	1789	Croat
Der Ladiner	1908 May 15	Tessmann
Der Landsturm	1915–1916	UHEID

155

Title	Dates	Key
Der Landsturm-Bote von Briey	1914 Oct–Nov	BNF
Der Lecha Patriot	1839–1959	Chron
Der Lecha Patriot und Northampton Demokrat	1839–1840; 1841–1847	Chron
Der Lechbote	1848–1851	OPACPlus
Der letzte Appell	1920	DHM
Der Liberale Beobachter und Berks, Montgomery und Schuylkill Counties Anzeiger	1839–1851	Chron
Der Liberale Beobachter und Northampton Caunty Wöchentlicher Anzeiger	1838–1839	Chron
Der Morgen	1925–1938	CompMem
Der Naabthal-Bote	1868	GooBook
Der Nationalsozialist	1921–1935 5 y; gaps	DHM
Der neue Anfang	1919	CompMem
Der neue Mahnruf	1948–2008	ANNO
Der Neue Teutsche Merkur	1790–1810	UBIEL
Der niederschlesische Anzeiger	1821–1822; 1826	ZEFYS
Der Nordstern	1877–1884	Chron
Der Odenwälder	1846–1852	UDARM
Der Oklahoma Courier	1894	OK Hist
Der Oldenburgische Volksfreund	1949–1952	UOLD
Der Omnibus	1848	GooBook

Title	Dates	Key
Der Orient	1840–1851	CompMem
Der Orientfrontkaempfer	1932–1934	BNF
Der Ostafrikanische Pflanzer	1909–1916	UFFM
Der österreichische Zuschauer	1836–1846	ANNO
Der Papierfabrikant	1914–1920	Hathi
Der Pilger	1842–1849	GooBook
Der Postbote aus Franken: eine Würzburger politische Zeitung	1832	GooBook
Der preußische Postfreund für Norddeutschland	1867–1868	GooBook
Der preußische Staatsanzeiger	1806	Bavarica
Der Proletarier	1919 Jul	DiFMOE
Der Proletarier	1924 Jul 30	DHM
Der Radikale	1849 Nov 4	DHM
Der Reichsbanner	1932	DHM
Der Reichsbote	1848–1849	DigiPress
Der Rheinbayer	1833–1835	GooBook
Der Rotthaler Bote	1872–1873	GooBook
Der Schnee	1905–1938	ANNO
Der Schweizer-Bote	1798, 1836–1842	GooBook
Der schweizerische Republikaner	1801	GooBook

Title	Dates	Key
Der Siebenbürger Bote	1785–1862	ANNO
Der Sonntag	1940 Apr 8	DHM
Der Spiegel	1947–present (latest year $)	Spiegel
Der Stahlhelm	1931 Sep 6	DHM
Der Standpunkt	1947–1957	Tessmann
Der Stürmer	1937	DHM
Der Tagesspiegel	1948–1950	CRL
Der Tägliche Demokrat	1917–1918	Chron
Der teutsche Reichs-Herold	1727	GooBook
Der Tiroler	1900–1925	Tessmann
Der Traunbote	1868–1869	UMUN
Der treue Zions-Wächter	1845–1854	CompMem
Der Umbruch	1940–1944	Liecht
Der Unpartheyische	1848	GooBook
Der unpartheyische Correspondent am Rhein	1794	UBONN
Der Volksbote	1894–1908; 1910–1933	FES
Der Volksfreund	1848	UBONN
Der Vorarlberger	1881–1892; 1917 -1927	ANNO
Der Vorarlberger Volksfreund	1893–1918 22 y; gaps	ANNO

Title	Dates	Key
Der Wächter am Rhein	1848–1849	UDUS
Der Wächter: Polizeiblatt für Mecklenburg	1838–1933 coming	Berlin
Der Wächter: Polizeiblatt für Mecklenburg	1871–1872	GooBook
Der Wähler	1896–1897	ANNO
Der Wahre Amerikaner	1804 Oct 11 - 1811 Dec 28	NewsBank
Der Wahrheitsfreund	1837–1858	Switz
Der Wahrheitsfreund	1838–1863 10 y; gaps	Hathi
Der Wanderer	1814–1873	ANNO
Der Weltbothe und wahre Republikaner von Berks, Montgomery und Schuylkill Counties	1814–1827	NewsBank
Der Wöchentliche Philadelphische Staatsbote	1872 Jan 18–1779 May 26	NewsBank
Der Zeitungs-Verlag	1906; 1920–1932; 1939–1942	ANNO
Deutsch-amerikanische Buchdrucker-Zeitung	1899–1928 9 y; gaps	GooBook
Deutsch-Amerikanischer Jugendfreund	1890 (title page, contents)	Ablit
Deutsch-chinesische Nachrichten	1930–1939	ZEFYS
Deutsche Auswanderer-Zeitung	1867	GooBook
Deutsche Bau-Zeitung	1867–1923	UCOT
Deutsche Brüsseler Zeitung	1847–1848	BelgLib
Deutsche Buchbinderzeitung	1880–1885	FES
Deutsche constitutionelle Zeitung	1848–1849	DigiPress

Title	Dates	Key
Deutsche demokratische Zeitung	1918–1921	UBONN
Deutsche Fleischbeschauer-Zeitung	1906	OpenLib
Deutsche Gemeinde-Zeitung	1870	GooBook
Deutsche Industri-Zeitung	1866	GooBook
Deutsche Israelitische Zeitung	1900–1938	Baeck
Deutsche Kolonialzeitung	1887–1908 10 y; gaps	GooBook
Deutsche Marokko-Zeitung	1907–1913	Humboldt
Deutsche Porcupein	1798 Jan 3	NewsBank
Deutsche Post	1915–1918	DiFMOE
Deutsche Reichs- und Gesetz-Zeitung	1797–1799	GooBook
Deutsche Schriftsteller-Zeitung	1910–1911	ZEFYS
Deutsche Uhrmacher-Zeitung	1879–1880; 1882–1942	UDRES
Deutsche Wacht	1883–1919	Slovenia
Deutsche Weinzeitung	1864–1865, 1867, 1872–1895	DiLibri
Deutsche Zeitung	1918	Euro
Deutsche Zeitung	1929–1937	Slovenia
Deutsche Zeitung	1847–1850	GooBook
Deutsche Zeitung Bohemia	1914–1938	Kram
Deutsche Zeitung für die Krim und Taurien	1918	UBERL

Title	Dates	Key
Deutsche Zeitung in Nordchina	1939–1941	ZEFYS
Deutsche Zeitung von Mexiko	1913 Feb 22; Mar 1	ZEFYS
Deutscher Beobachter oder Hanseatische privilegirte Zeitung	1816	GooBook
Deutscher Reichs-Anzeiger	1872–1873	GooBook
Deutsches Bauernblatt	1919 March 1	DiFMOE
Deutsches Kolonialblatt	1901	GooBook
Deutsches Kunstblatt	1850–1858	UHEID
Deutsches Nordmährerblatt	1902–1916	ANNO
Deutsches Südmährisches Blatt	1911	ANNO
Deutsches Tageblatt	1886 Aug	UHEID
Deutsches Tageblatt	1919 Feb March	DiFMOE
Deutsches Volksblatt	1889–1922	ANNO
Deutsches Wochenblatt	1917–1919	Hathi
Deutsches Wochenblatt für constitutionelle Monarchie	1849–1851	DigiPress
Deutsch-Kroner Zeitung	1886 Aug	UHEID
Deutsch-Ostafrikanische Zeitung	1899–1916	Berlin
Diarium Hebdomadale, oder wöchentliche auiso	1620	UBREM
Dibre Emeth	1845–1906	CompMem
Didaskalia: Blätter für Geist, Gemüth und Publizität	1830; 1839	GooBook

Title	Dates	Key
Die Arbeit	1885–1886	ANNO
Die Arbeit	1894–1921	ANNO
Die Arbeit	1924–1933	FES
Die Arbeiterin	1928–1931	ANNO
Die Arbeiterinnen-Zeitung	1892–1902; 1910–1919	ANNO
Die Aurora	1876 Jun	UGOT
Die bayerische Landwehr	1916–1918	USTR
Die Betriebsgemeinschaft der Leipziger Funkgerätebau	1940–1941; 1944	DHM
Die Bewegung	1936; 1942–1944	UHEID
Die Bombe	1871–1925	ANNO
Die braune Sonntagszeitung	1933–1934 limited	DigiPress
Die Brennnessel	1877	DiLibri
Die Bühne	1924–1943	ANNO
Die Debatte und Wiener Lloyd	1864–1869	Euro
Die Deutsche Zucker-Industrie: Wochenblatt	1907	Hathi
Die Donau	1940–1944	DiFMOE
Die Drogisten-Zeitung	1886–1943	ANNO
Die Fackel	1899–1936	AAS
Die Fackel	1914–1918	UFFM

Title	Dates	Key
Die Feder	1898–1917	ZEFYS
Die Film-Welt	1919; 1921–1925	ANNO
Die freie Meinung	1919–1932	Poland
Die Freie Zeitung	1917	Hathi
Die Freistatt	1913–1914	CompMem
Die Gegenwart	1897–1906	UKLN
Die Gemeinde	1914	UFFM
Die Grenzboten	1841–1848	GooBook
Die Grüne	1950–1980 (search only)	Hathi
Die Judenfrage	1886 Aug	UHEID
Die Kämpferin	1932	DHM
Die Karpathen-Post	1880–1942	DiFMOE
Die Kino-Woche	1919–1921	ANNO
Die Kommunistin	1919	DHM
Die KPD	1923	DHM
Die Kreatur	1926–1930	CompMem
Die literarische Praxis	1901–1902; 1905–1910	ZEFYS
Die Lokomotive	1904–1943	ANNO
Die Mährisch-Schlesische Presse	1892–1917	ANNO

Title	Dates	Key
Die Mauer	1917	UHEID
Die Muskete	1905–1941	ANNO
Die neue Mainzer Zeitung	1793	GooBook
Die neue Welt	1927–1938	CompMem
Die neue Zeit	1849	Euro
Die neue Zeitung	1907–1934	ANNO
Die Neuzeit	1861–1903 37 y; gaps	ANNO
Die Nürnberger Estaffette	1835	OPACPlus
Die Nutz- und Lust-erweckende Gesellschafft Der Vertrauten Nachbarn am Isarstrom	1868–1869	BavLib
Die Ostschweiz	1874–1900	Switz
Die Patrulle	1916	USTR
Die Post aus Deutschland	1918–1934	ZEFYS
Die Presse	1848–1896	Euro
Die Redaktion	1902–1916	ZEFYS
Die Rheinische Volks-Halle	1848 Dec 16	Euro
Die Rheinpfalz	1869	GooBook
Die rote Fahne	1918–1919, 1928–1933	ZEFYS
Die rote Fahne	1918–1939	ANNO
Die Rote Front	1927	DHM

Title	Dates	Key
Die Sappe	1915–1918	USTR
Die Schwarze Fahne	1925	DHM
Die Schwarze Front	1932 May	DHM
Die Somme-Wacht	1917	UHEID
Die Sonntags-Zeitung	1932	DHM
Die Spinnmaschine	1938; 1940	DHM
Die Stimme [Alte Folge]	1928–1938	CompMem
Die Stimme [Neue Folge]	1947–1966	CompMem
Die Uhrmacher-Woche	1914–1942	UDRES
Die Union	1866–1867	TX Hist
Die Vedette	1871	ANNO
Die Volkspost	1926–1934	ANNO
Die Voss	1921–1925	CRL
Die Wacht im Osten	1916	UHEID
Die Wacht im Westen	1917	UHEID
Die Wage	1848–1852	Lippe
Die Wählerin	1918–1919	ANNO
Die Wahrheit	1899–1938	CompMem
Die Welt	1897–1914	CompMem

Title	Dates	Key
Die Zeit	1902–1919	ANNO
Die Zeit	1946–present	CompMem
Dinkelsbühlisches Intelligenzblatt	1797–1799	GooBook
Dolomiten	1923–1943	Tessmann
Donau-Armee-Zeitung	1917	UBERL
Donau-Zeitung	1851–1852; 1858; 1862	GooBook
Dörptsche Zeitung	1791, 1804–1864	Euro
Dr. Blochs Österreichische Wochenschrift	1891–1920	CompMem
Dramaturgisches Wochenblatt	1815–1817	UMST
Dresdner Anzeiger	1886 Aug	UHEID
Dresdner Journal	1886 Aug	UHEID
Dresdner Journal	1906 Jan 1–2	WikiS
Dresdner Morgenzeitung	1827	GooBook
Dresdner Nachrichten	1886 Aug	UHEID
Dresdner Zeitung	1945	Euro
Dresdner Zeitung	1838; 1840–1843	ANNO
Dresdner Zeitung	1886 Aug	UHEID
Duisburger Intelligenz-Zeitung	1739–1768	Blank
Düna-Zeitung	1916–1918	BNF

Title	Dates	Key
Dürener Anzeiger und Unterhaltungsblatt	1855–1856	UBONN
Dürener Zeitung	1886; 1889; 1896–1919	UBONN
Düsseldorfer Erzähler	1818; 1822	UDUS
Düsseldorfer Intelligenz- und Adreß-Blatt	1824–1825	UDUS
Düsseldorfer Literarisch-Merkantilisches Intelligenz- und Adreß-Blatt	1825–1826	UDUS
Düsseldorfer Zeitung	1886 Aug	UHEID
Echo der Gegenwart	1886	UHEID
Echo der Gegenwart	1886 Aug	UHEID
Egerer Anzeiger	1847–1868	Portafont
Egerer Zeitung	1868–1900	Portafont
Eggenburger Zeitung	1914–1919	ANNO
Ehrenbreitsteiner Intelligenzblatt	1838	UBONN
Eichsfelder Generalanzeiger	coming	HIgnst
Eichsfelder Tageblatt	coming	HIgnst
Eichsfelder Volksblätter	1864–coming	HIgnst
Eichsfeldia	1884–1924 coming	HIgnst
Eichstätter Intelligenzblatt	1810–1812; 1823; 1828	GooBook
Eichstätter Tagblatt	1864	GooBook
Eisenbahn-Zeitung	1832–1850 12 y; gaps	GooBook

Title	Dates	Key
Eisenbergisches Nachrichtenblatt	1821–1830	UJENA
Eiserne Front	1932	DHM
el	1844–1846	ZEFYS
Elberfelder Intelligenzblatt	1827–1828; 1838–1840	UBONN
Elberfelder Zeitung	1886 Aug	UHEID
Elbinger Anzeiger	1918–1945	Elblag
Elbinger Volksblatt	1870	Euro
Elsässer Kurier	1897; 1914–1917	BNF
Elsässer Tagblatt	1889; 1913–1918	BNF
Elsäss-Lothringisches Schulblatt	1871; 1914–1918	BNF
Entomologische Zeitung	1842–1911	Bio
Erdöl-Zeitung	1950–1955	Sweden
Erfa, Kreis-Intelligenzblatt für Euskirchen, Rheinbach und Ahrweiler	1840–1847	UBONN
Erfurtisches Intelligenz-Blatt	1769–1771; 1773	GooBook
Erlanger Mittwochs-Blatt	1835	GooBook
Erlanger Real-Zeitung	1820	GooBook
Erlanger Tagblatt	1863–1865	GooBook
Erlanger Zeitung	1827–1829	GooBook
Ermländische Zeitung	1902, 1904–1905	ZEFYS

Title	Dates	Key
Erste allgemeine öster. Hebammen-Zeitung	1887–1888	ANNO
Es muss Tag werden	1848–1849	DigiPress
Esra	1919–1920	CompMem
Etwas von gelehrten Rostockschen Sachen	1737–1748	UROS
Europe Speaks	1940–1947	FES
Extract der eingelauffenen Nouvellen	1742–1744, 1746, 1748	ZEFYS
Fehrbelliner Zeitung	1925–1941	ZEFYS
Feldkircher Anzeiger	1866–1939 71 y; gaps	ANNO
Feldkircher Wochenblatt	1810–1857	ANNO
Feldzeitung der Armee-Abteilung Scheffer	1918	UHEID
Fest-Zeitung	1890	UBONN
Feuilles d'affiches annonces et avis divers de Bonn	1812–1814	UBONN
Feuilleton zum Pfälzischer Kurier	1868–1871; 1873	Bavarica
Fliegende Blätter	1844–1944	UHEID
Flora	1818–1902	UREG
Flörsheimer Zeitung	1906–1932	RheinMain
Flugblatt	1849	UBONN
Frankensteiner Kreisblatt	1877–1896	ZEFYS
Frankensteiner Wochenblatt	1836–1842	ZEFYS

Title	Dates	Key
Frankenthaler Wochen-Blatt	1823–1828	GooBook
Frankenzeitung	1863	GooBook
Frankfurt-Bockenheimer Anzeige-Blatt	1914	UFFM
Frankfurter Aerzte-Correspondenz	1913–1918	UFFM
Frankfurter Bürgerzeitung Sonne	1914	UFFM
Frankfurter Illustrierte	1942	UDARM
Frankfurter Israelitisches Familienblatt	1902–1923	CompMem
Frankfurter Journal	1886 Aug	UHEID
Frankfurter Konversationsblatt	1834; 1840–1852	GooBook
Frankfurter Nachrichten	1857–1865 7 y; gaps	Hathi
Frankfurter Nachrichten und Intelligenzblatt	1914	UFFM
Frankfurter Oberpostamts-Zeitung	1814–1849 26 y; gaps	GooBook
Frankfurter Universitäts-Zeitung	1914–1919	UFFM
Frankfurter Zeitung	1886 Aug	UHEID
Frankfurter Zeitung und Handelsblatt	1914	UFFM
Frankfurter Zeitung und Handelsblatt	1866–1943	CRL
Fränkische Provinzialblätter	1802–1804	GooBook
Fränkische Zeitung	1863	GooBook
Fränkischer Anzeiger	1870–1873	GooBook

Title	Dates	Key
Fränkischer Kurier	1852–1873	GooBook
Fränkischer Merkur	1814; 1838–1839; 1843	GooBook
Fränkischer Wald	1859; 1871; 1907–1936	GooBook
Fränkisches Bürgerblatt	1848	DigiPress
Frauenblätter	1871–1872	ANNO
Freiburger Nachrichten	1864–1920	RERO
Freiburger Wochenblatt	1818	GooBook
Freiburger Zeitung und Anzeiger für die westliche Schweiz	1864–1903	UFRBG
Freie Tribüne	1919–1921	CompMem
Freies Deutschland	1848 Apr 12	DHM
Freiheitsbothe	1810 Feb 14	NewsBank
Freimaurer-Zeitung	1876	GooBook
Freimunds Kirchlidh-Politisches Wochenblatt für Stadt und Land	1839; 1857	GooBook
Freisinger Tagblatt	1868–1942; 1949–1968	UMUN
Freisinger Tagblatt	1871–1873	GooBook
Fremden-Blatt	1847; 1849–1855; 1913–1919	ANNO
Freyheits-Fahne	1814 Aug 27 - 1817 Mar 25	NewsBank
Freymaurer-Zeitung	1786	UBONN
Freysinger Wochenblatt	1849	GooBook

Title	Dates	Key
Fuldaisches Intelligenz-Blatt	1804–1815	UFULD
Fürstlich Reuß-plauisches Amts-und Verordnungsblatt	1836–1842	GooBook
Fürstlich Waldeckisches Regierungsblatt	1837	BavLib
Fürstlich Waldeckisches Regierungsblatt, -blätter	1853–1869, 1880–1908	Hathi
Fürstlich Waldeckisches Regierungsblätter	1853–1908 37 y; gaps	Hathi
Fürstlich-Lippisches Regierungs- und Anzeigeblatt	1843–1871	NRW Lib
Fürtenfeldbrucker Zeitung	1928–1939; 1942; 1944–1945	DigiPress
Fürther Abendzeitung	1845	GooBook
Fürther Tagblatt	1838–1934	OPACPlus
Fürther Tagblatt	1849	GooBook
Fürther Tagblatt/Erzähler	1918	DHM
Fürther Tagblatt/Erzähler	1851–1896	OPACPlus
Fussball-Zeitung	1937–1940	ANNO
Garten-Zeitung	1883–1885	Bio
Gazette des Ardennes	1914–1918	UHEID
Gebweilerer Wochenblatt	1870–1871	Hathi
Gefolgschaft Pittler	1943	DHM
Gemeindeblatt der Israelitischen Gemeinde Frankfurt am Main	1922–1938	CompMem
Gemeinnütziges Hausarchiv	1807–1808	UMST

Title	Dates	Key
Gemeinnütziges Justiz- und Polizeiblatt der Teutschen	1810	UJENA
Gemeinnütziges Wochenblatt für Geilenkirchen und Umgegend	1836–1837	UBONN
Gemeinnütziges Wochenblatt für Geilenkirchen, Heinsberg und Umgegend	1838–1866 16 y; gaps	UBONN
General Staatsbothe	1811 Dec 27	NewsBank
General-Anzeiger	1886 Aug	UHEID
General-Anzeiger für Berlinchen, Bernstein und Umgegend	1923	GooBook
General-Anzeiger für Deutschland	1872	GooBook
General-Anzeiger für Stadt und Kreis Düren	1891–1895	UBONN
General-Gouvernements-Blatt fur Sachsen	1813–1815	Berlin
General-Gouvernements-Blatt fur das Königlich Preussische Herzogthum Sachsen	1815–1816	Berlin
Gerdauener Zeitung	1896	ARCOR
Gerichts-Halle	1871	ANNO
Germania	1886 Aug	UHEID
Geschäfts- und Unterhaltungsblatt für den Kreis Grevenbroich und dessen Umgebung	1863, 1865–1866	UBONN
Gesetzblatt für das Königreich Bayern	1818–1872 35 y; gaps	Hathi
Gesetzes- und Verordnungsblatt für das Großherzogthum Baden	1901–1903, 1909, 1911	Hathi
Gewerkschaftliche Rundschau	1923–1933	FES
Gewissen	1919–1929	ZEFYS

Title	Dates	Key
Gießener Anzeiger	1886 Aug	UHEID
Gnädigst privilegierte Bönnisches Intelligenz-Blatt	1772–1775; 1785–1792	UBONN
Gnädigst privilegirtes Altenburgisches Intelligenz-Blatt	1818–1819	GooBook
Goldaper Kreisblatt	1908–1914; 1916–1929	ZEFYS
Goldingenscher Anzeiger	1911–1915; 1929–1930	Latvia
Görlitzer Anzeiger	1818–1868 9 y; many gaps	ZEFYS
Görlitzer Fama	1842; 1847–1849	ZEFYS
Gothaische gelehrte Zeitungen	1781	ANNO
Göttingische gelehrte Anzeigen	1772–1845 10 y; gaps	GooBook
Göttingische Zeitung von gelehrten Sachen	1739–1752	UCLAU
Göttingsche Policey-Amts Nachrichten	1765–1767	UBIEL
Gottscheer Bote	1904–1915	ANNO
Gradaus mein deutsches Volk!	1848–1849	DigiPress
Grafinger Zeitung	1923–1949 22 y; gaps	DigiPress
Graphische Presse	1889–1917	FES
Graphische Stimme	1905–1933	FES
Grätzer Zeitung	1845	GooBook
Grazer Mittags-Zeitung	1914–1921	ANNO

Title	Dates	Key
Grazer Tagblatt	1892–1923	ANNO
Grazer Volksblatt	1868–1900; 1905–1911	ANNO
Grazer Zeitung	1775; 1812–1848	ANNO
Greifenhagener Kreisblatt	1844–1850	Berlin
Greifenhagener Kreisblatt	1844–1850	ZEFYS
Greifenhagener Kreiszeitung	1915–1921	ZEFYS
Greifswaldisches Wochen-Blatt von allerhand gelehrten und nützlichen Sachen	1743	UGOT
Grevenbroicher Kreisblatt	1855–1869 8 y; gaps	UBONN
Grevenbroicher Kreisblatt und landwirthschaftlicher Anzeiger für das Jülicher Land	1861–1863	UBONN
Grevenbroicher Kreisblatt und Organ für die Gilbach	1858–1859	UBONN
Grevesmühlener Wochenblatt	1851–1868	UROS
Grönenbacher Wochenblatt	1859	GooBook
Großenhainer Unterhaltungs- und Anzeigeblatt	1847–1859	UDRES
Großherzoglich badisches Amts- und Regierungsblatt für den Oberrhein-Kreis	1839–1855	GooBook
Großherzoglich badisches Anzeigeblatt für den Seekreis	1848	GooBook
Großherzoglich Badisches niederrheinisches Provinzialblatt	1808–1810	UHEID
Großherzoglich Mecklenburgisch-Strelitzer officieler Anzeiter für Gesetzgebung und Staatsverwaltung	1870–1873	GooBook
Großherzoglich Sachsen-Weimar-Eisenachisches Regierungs-Blatt	1817–1836	UJENA

175

Title	Dates	Key
Großherzoglich-Badisches Regierungs-Blatt	1831–1868	Hathi
Großherzoglich-Badisches Staats- und Regierungs-Blatt	1803–1844	Hathi
Gross-Strehlitzer Kreisblatt	1915–1926	ZEFYS
Gross-Wartenberger Kreisblatt	1908–1925	ZEFYS
Grottkauer Stadt- und Kreisblatt	1841–1845	Poland
Grottkauer Zeitung	1883–1939 46 y; gaps	Poland
Grünberger Wochenblatt	1848;1875	Euro
Grünberger Wochenblatt	1857–1863	ZEFYS
Gründliche Warhafftige Newe Zeitung	1626	BavLib
Guhrauer Anzeiger	1914–1917	ZEFYS
Gülich und bergische wöchentliche Nachrichten	1769–1802	UDUS
Gumbinner Kreisblatt	1907–1914; 1925–1930	ZEFYS
Gummersbacher Kreisblatt	1836–1852	UBONN
Guttentager Stadtblatt	1907–1921	Poland
Habelschwerdter Kreisblatt	1843–1848; 1907–1909	Berlin
Hagenauer Zeitung	1882; 1912–1918	BNF
Hallisches Tageblatt	1828–1845; 1847	Hathi
Hallisches Wochenblatt	1828–1847	Hathi

Title	Dates	Key
Hamburger Abendblatt	1948–present	Abendblatt
Hamburger Anzeiger	1888–1944	Euro
Hamburger Börsenhalle	1805–1904	Euro
Hamburger Fremdenblatt	1886 Aug	UHEID
Hamburger Garten- und Blumenzeitung	1852–1890 17 y; gaps	Bio
Hamburger Musikalische Zeitung	1837–1838	GooBook
Hamburger Nachrichten	1792–1939	Euro
Hamburger Zeitung	1943; 1944–1945	Euro
Hamburgischer Correspondent	1886 Aug	UHEID
Hamburgischer Correspondent (coming)	1721–1934	Euro
Hamburgisches Gesetz- und Verordnungsblatt	1906–1920	Hathi
Hamburgisches Gesetz- und Verordnungsblatt	1921–1922	Hathi
Hammsches Wochenblatt	1824	UMST
Hanauer neue europäische Zeitung	1797	GooBook
Handels-Zeitung für die gesamte Uhren-Industrie	1898	UDRES
Handlungsgehülfen-Blatt	1897–1918	FES
Hannoverscher Courier	1867–1869	ZEFYS
Hannoverscher Courier	1886 Aug	UHEID
Hannoversches Tagblatt	1886 Aug	UHEID

Title	Dates	Key
Hausangestellten-Zeitung	1909–1932	FES
Hebammen-Zeitung	1891	ANNO
Heidelberger Neueste Nachrichten	1936	UHEID
Heidelberger Tagblatt	1848–1860	UHEID
Heidelberger Zeitung	1861–1867; 1903–1905; 1919	UHEID
Heinsberger Kreisblatt	1857–1868	UBONN
Helmstedter Kreisblatt	1934 May 1	GooBook
Henneberger Zeitung	1871–1919	UJENA
Hennefer Volkszeitung	1892–1939 42 y; gaps	Hennef
Hermanner Zeitung	1875–1922	Chron
Herold des Glaubens	1838–1839; 1841	GooBook
Herzogl. Sachsen-Coburgisches Regierungs- und Intelligenzblatt	1826–1839	DigiPress
Herzogl. Sachsen-Coburg-Saalfeldes Regierungs- und Intelligenzblatt	1807–1825	GooBook
Herzoglich Mecklenburg-Schwerinisches officieles Wochenblatt	1812–1815	Hathi
Herzoglich Mecklenburg-Schwerinisches officieles Wochenblatt	1814; 1829	GooBook
Herzoglich nassauisches allgemeines Intelligenzblatt	1819	GooBook
Hessische Gemeindebeamten-Zeitung	1923	UDARM
Hessische landwirtschaftliche Zeitschrift	1845–1865	Hathi

Title	Dates	Key
Hessische Morgenzeitung	1886 Aug	UHEID
Hessisch-Nassauischer Volksbote	1914–1919	UFFM
HJ im Vormarsch	1938	ZEFYS
Hochheimer Stadtanzeiger	1911–1932	RheinMain
Hochzeits-Zeitung	1902	Euro
Hofer Zeitung	1868	GooBook
Holsteinische Stände-Zeitung	1857	GooBook
Hunsrücker Erzähler	1905; 1907	DiLibri
Illlustrirtes Familien-Journal	1855–1856	AustLit
Illustrierte Garten-Zeitung	1861–1875	Bio
Illustrierte Sonntags-Zeitung	1895–1917	UBONN
Illustrierte Wochenbeilage der Schlesischen Zeitung	1924–1934	Poland
Illustrierter Sonntag	1929–1931	DigiPress
Illustriertes Sonntags-Blatt	1899–1916	UFFM
Illustriertes Familienblatt	1913; 1925–1938	ANNO
Illustriertes Unterhaltungs-Blatt	1875–1899; 1901–1917	UDARM
Illustriertes Wiener Extrablatt	1902–1903	ANNO
Illustrirte Monatshefte	1865–1866	CompMem
Illustrirte Zeitung	1841–1873	GooBook

Title	Dates	Key
Im Deutschen Reich	1895–1922	CompMem
Im Schützengraben in den Vogesen	1915–1916	USTR
Indiana Tribüne	1900–1907	IndHS
Ingolstädter Anzeiger	1920; 1922–1933	DigiPress
Ingolstädter Tagblatt	1873	GooBook
Ingolstädter Wochen-Blatt	1839–1868 26 ; gaps	GooBook
Ingolstädter Zeitung	1920, 1922–1933	DigiPress
Innsbrucker Nachrichten	1860–1903	Euro
Innsbrucker Zeitung	1954–1919	ANNO
Innviertler Heimatblatt	1939–1943	ANNO
Innzeitung	1862–1866	Tessmann
Intelligenz-Blatt	1856	Sandusky
Intelligenz-Blatt der freien Stadt Frankfurt	1864	ArchOrg
Intelligenz-Blatt der freien Stadt Frankfurt	1750–1864 40 y; major gaps	GooBook
Intelligenz-Blatt der freien Stadt Frankfurt	1750–1864 71 y; gaps	Hathi
Intelligenzblatt der Jenaischen allgemeinen Literatur-Zeitung	1803–1842	ArchOrg
Intelligenzblatt der königlich baierischen Stadt Kempten	1827	GooBook
Intelligenzblatt der Königlich bayerischen Stadt Nördlingen	1816; 1818–1819	GooBook
Intelligenzblatt der Königlichen Bayerischen Stadt Nördlingen	1815–1841	GooBook

Title	Dates	Key
Intelligenz-Blatt der königlichen Regierung von Schwaben und Neuburg	1838	GooBook
Intelligenzblatt der Reichsstadt Lindau	1783–1787	GooBook
Intelligenzblatt des königlich baierischen Iller-Kreises	1811–1816	GooBook
Intelligenzblatt des pharmaceutischen Vereins in Baiern	1827	GooBook
Intelligenzblatt des Rezat-Kreises	1817; 1825; 1835	GooBook
Intelligenz-Blatt des Rheinkreises	1818–1830	GooBook
Intelligenzblatt für das Königreich Bayern	1819–1820; 1825	GooBook
Intelligenzblatt für den Kreis Bingen	1837	UDARM
Intelligenz-Blatt für den Kreis Simmen	1843–1846	UBONN
Intelligenz-Blatt für den Kreis Simmen und dessen Umge	1847–1856; 1859–1862	UBONN
Intelligenzblatt für die Provinz Oberhessen	1833–1934	UDARM
Intelligenzblatt für die Stadt Bern	1834–1922	U BERN
Intelligenzblatt für die Städte Oels, Bernstadt, Juliusburg, Hundsfeld und Festenberg	1856–1859	ZEFYS
Intelligenzblatt für Kunst und Literatur	1808; 1823–1824	Bavarica
Intelligenzblatt für Nassau	1868	GooBook
Intelligenzblatt für Unterfranken und Aschaffenburg	1851; 1855–1856	GooBook
Intelligenz-Blatt und wöchentlicher Anzeiger der königlich bairischen Stadt Augsburg	1819–1872 7 y; major gaps	GooBook
Intelligenzblatt von täglichen Vorkommenheiten in Pommern und Rügen	1753–1757	UGRF

Title	Dates	Key
Intelligenzblatt von Unterfranken und Aschaffenburg	1841; 1851; 1861	GooBook
Intelligenzblatt zur deutschen Zeitung	1789–1790	SPO
Ischler Bade-Liste	1861	ANNO
ISIS, oder, Enzyclopaedische Zeitung von Oken	1818–1819	Bio
Israelitische Annalen	1849–1841	CompMem
Israelitische Religionsgesellschaft Frankfurt a.M.	1864–1929 58 y; gaps	CompMem
Israelitische Rundschau	1901–1902	CompMem
Israels Herold	1849	Hathi
ITF	1929–1933	FES
Jahrbuch der Gesellschaft der Geschichte der Juden in der Čechoslowakischen Republik	1929–1938	CompMem
Jahrbuch der Jüdisch-Literarischen Gesellschaft	1903–1932	CompMem
Jahrbuch für die Geschichte der Juden und des Judenthums	1860–1862; 1869	CompMem
Jahrbuch für jüdische Geschichte und Literatur	1898–1937 33 y; gaps	CompMem
Jahrbücher für jüdische Geschichte und Literatur	1874–1890 9 y; gaps	CompMem
Jahresbericht der K. Studienanstalt zu Kaiserslautern	1824	GooBook
Jahresbericht der königlichen Bewerbschule in Wunsiedel	1867; 1869–1870; 1873	GooBook
Jahresbericht der Königlichen Gewerb- und Handelsschule zu Fürth	1853; 1864; 1870	GooBook
Jahresbericht der königlichen Gewerbschule zu Kissingen	1873	GooBook

Title	Dates	Key
Jahresbericht der Königlichen Kreisackerbauschule	1861	GooBook
Jahresbericht der Königlichen Landwirthschafts- und Gewerbsschule zu Schweinfurt	1853–1855; 1869	GooBook
Jahresbericht der königlichen Studienschule zu Memmingen	1823	GooBook
Jahresbericht der lateinischen Vorbereitungsschulen zu Erlangen	1824	GooBook
Jahresbericht der Lateinschule zu Thurnau	1864	GooBook
Jahresbericht der Niederösterreichischen Ober-Realschule	1869–1870; 1906	GooBook
Jahresbericht der Realschule erster Ordnung zu Siegen	1865	GooBook
Jahresbericht der Schulen des Frauenerwerb-Vereins	1907–1918	ANNO
Jahresbericht des deutschen Wohltätigkeits-Vereins St. Petersburg	1872	GooBook
Jahresbericht des Entomologischen Vereins von Stettin	1839	Bio
Jahresbericht des Gymnasiums zu Zwickau	1872	GooBook
Jahresbericht des K. K. Gymnasiums zu Pilsen	1863–1865; 1867–1868	GooBook
Jahresbericht des K. K. Ober-Gymnasiums in Görz	1856	GooBook
Jahresbericht des Königl. kath. Gymnasiums zu Neisse	1873	GooBook
Jahresbericht des Königl. Katholischen Gymnasiums zu Glatz	1840; 1843	GooBook
Jahresbericht des Königlichen Gymnasiums und des Realgymnasiums zu Hamm	1908	GooBook
Jahresbericht des Königlichen Gymnasiums zu Lyck	1901	GooBook
Jahresbericht des Königlichen Gymnasiums zu Wongrowitz	1874	GooBook
Jahresbericht des Königlichen Katholischen Gymnasium zu Groß-Glogau	1843–1907 9 y; gaps	GooBook

Title	Dates	Key
Jahresbericht des königlichen katholischen Gymnasiums an Marzellen zu Cöln	1863	GooBook
Jahresbericht des königlichen katholischen Gymnasiums zu Gleiwitz	1873	GooBook
Jahresbericht des königlichen katholischen Gymnasiums zu Oppeln	1902	GooBook
Jahresbericht des Lyceums 1 zu Hannover	1874	GooBook
Jahresbericht des Mädchen-Lyzeums am Kohlmarkt	1902–1913	ANNO
Jahresbericht des Mädchen-Lyzeums der Stadt Znaim	1906–1919	ANNO
Jahresbericht des N. ö. Landes-Realgymnasiums in Klosterneuburg	1936	GooBook
Jahresbericht des städtischen Gymnasiums zu Neustadt Ob.-Schl.	1873	GooBook
Jahresbericht des Vereins für erweiterte Frauenbildung in Wien	1888–1914	ANNO
Jahresbericht für die Landwirthschafts- und Gewerbsschule zu Schwabach	1838	GooBook
Jahresbericht über das grossh. Lyceum zu Heidelberg	1867	GooBook
Jahresbericht über das Gymnasium Celle	1888; 1893; 1897	GooBook
Jahresbericht über das Gymnasium Dionysianum zu Rheine	1868;1873	GooBook
Jahresbericht über das Gymnasium und die Lateinische Schule zu Speyer	1838; 1869	GooBook
Jahresbericht über das Gymnasium zu Prenzlau	1831	GooBook
Jahresbericht über das Gymnasium zu Sorau	1864; 1868; 1873	GooBook
Jahresbericht über das Königlich Katholische Gymnasium zu Braunsberg	1859	GooBook
Jahresbericht über das Königliche Gymnasium und die Vorschule zu Saarbrücken	1874	GooBook
Jahresbericht über das Königliche Gymnasium zu Duisburg	1850–1851; 1873	GooBook

Title	Dates	Key
Jahresbericht über das Königliche Gymnasium zu Rinteln	1847	GooBook
Jahresbericht über das Königliche katholische Gymnasium zu Leobschütz	1883	GooBook
Jahresbericht über das Königliche Progymnasium zu Rothenburg	1854; 1870	GooBook
Jahresbericht über das Kurfürstliche Gymnasium zu Hanau	1849	GooBook
Jahresbericht über das Schuljahr 1873–1874	1874; 1901	GooBook
Jahresbericht über das Schuljahr von Ostern 1878–Ostern 1879	1879	GooBook
Jahresbericht über das Schwarzburgische Gymnasium zu Sondershausen	1845–1846	GooBook
Jahresbericht über die Fürstl.-Leining. Lateinschule zu Amorbach	1873	GooBook
Jahresbericht über die Gewerbschule Amberg	1865	GooBook
Jahresbericht über die höhere Knaben-Schule	1870	GooBook
Jahresbericht über die K. Bayer. Lateinschule zu Hassfurt	1859–1860	GooBook
Jahresbericht über die Kgl. Bayerische Katholische Lateinschule zu Kitzingen	1864	GooBook
Jahresbericht über die kgl. Bayerische Studienanstalt in Burghausen	1873	GooBook
Jahresbericht über die kgl. Bayerische Studienanstalt in Edenkoben	1837–1858	GooBook
Jahresbericht über die Königl. Bayer. Lateinische Schule zu Kirchheimbolanden	1895	GooBook
Jahresbericht über die Königl. Bayer. Lateinschule zu Miltenberg a. M.	1854	GooBook
Jahresbericht über die Königlich Bayerische Lateinschule in Günzbug	1863	GooBook
Jahresbericht über die königlich Bayerische Lateinschule in Hammelburg	1872	GooBook
Jahresbericht über die Königlich Bayerische Lateinschule zu Homburg in der Pfalz	1842	GooBook

Title	Dates	Key
Jahresbericht über die Königliche Bayerische Lateinische Schule . . . Frankenthal	1869	GooBook
Jahresbericht über die Königliche Bayerische Lateinschule . . . Germersheim	1860–1873 10 y; gaps	GooBook
Jahresbericht über die königliche Gewerbschule in Traunstein	1873	GooBook
Jahresbericht über die königliche Gewerbschule zu Straubing	1870; 1873; 1876–1877	GooBook
Jahresbericht über die Königliche lateinschule zu Nördlingen	1848	GooBook
Jahresbericht über die Königliche Realschule zu Weißenburg a. Sd.	1872	GooBook
Jahresbericht über die Königliche Studien-Anstalt in Münnerstadt	1861	GooBook
Jahresbericht über die lateinische Schule Blieskastel	1840	GooBook
Jahresbericht über die lateinische Schule im Benediktiner-Stifte Metten	1844	GooBook
Jahresbericht über die Lateinische Schule zu Cusel	1841	GooBook
Jahresbericht über die Lateinische Schule zu Dürkheim	1838	GooBook
Jahresbericht über die Lateinische Schule zu Hersbruck	1873	GooBook
Jahresbericht über die Lateinische Schule zu Kaufbeuren	1867	GooBook
Jahresbericht über die nied. Österr. Landes-Oberrealschule in Krems	1865	GooBook
Jahresbericht über die Realschule Barmen	1872	GooBook
Jahresbericht von dem Königlichen Progymnasium zu Grünstadt im Rheinkreise	1820–1824	GooBook
Jahresbericht von der Königlichen Studien-Anstalt zu Dillingen	1820; 1822; 1827	GooBook
Jahresbericht von der Lateinischen Stadtschule in Landsberg im Isarkreis	1832	GooBook
Jahresbericht von der lateinischen Vorbereitungsschule in Neustadt a. d. Haardt	1827	GooBook

Title	Dates	Key
Jahresbericht von Ostern 1863 bis dahin 1864 (Gymnasium Eisleben)	1864	GooBook
Jahresbericht. Evangelisches Städtisches Gymnasium zu Lauban	1896	GooBook
Jahresberichte der Jacobson-Schule	1867–1928; 1930–1931	CompMem
Jahresberichte der Landes-Rabinnerschule in Budapest	1878–1918	CompMem
Jahresberichte der Verwaltungsbehöirgen der freien Stadt Hamburg	1906	Hathi
Jahresberichte des jüdisch-theologischen Seminars Fraenkelische Stiftung	1854; 1856–1937	CompMem
Jenaer Literaturzeitung	1874–1876	UJENA
Jenaer Volksblatt	1896–1941	UJENA
Jenaische Beyträge zur neuesten gelehrten Gechichte	1757	UJENA
Jenaische gelehrte Anzeigen	1787	UJENA
Jenaische gelehrte Zeitungen	1749–1786	UCLAU
Jenaische Nachrichten von Gelehrten und andere Sachen	1747	UJENA
Jenaische Zeitung	1872–1945	UJENA
Jeschurun (Alte Folge)	1854–1869; 1883–1887	CompMem
Jeschurun (Neue Folge)	1914–1930	CompMem
Journal des Nieder- und Mittelrheins	1814–1816	UDUS
Journal des österreichischen Lloyd	1841	ANNO
Journal für Ornithologie	1853–1921	Bio
Journal für Prediger	1770–1802	GooBook

Title	Dates	Key
Journal von und für Deutschland	1784–1792	UBIEL
Judaica	1934–1937	CompMem
Jüdische Allgemeine	1946– ?	Jud Allg
Jüdische Arbeits- und Wanderfürsorge	1927–1929	CompMem
Jüdische Korrespondenz	1915–1920	CompMem
Jüdische Presse	1920–1938	CompMem
Jüdische Rundschau	1902–1938	CompMem
Jüdische Schulzeitung	1925–1938	CompMem
Jüdische Volksstimme	1912–1920	CompMem
Jüdische Welt-Rundschau	1939–1940	CompMem
Jüdische Zeitschrift für Wissenschaft und Leben	1862–1872; 1875	CompMem
Jüdische Zeitung	1807–1920	CompMem
Jüdisches Jahrbuch für die Schweiz	1916–1922	CompMem
Jüdisches Jahrbuch für Sachsen	1931–1932	CompMem
Jüdisches Volksblatt	1899–1905	CompMem
Jüdisch-liberale Zeitung	1920–1938	CompMem
Jugend	1896–1940	UHEID
Jugend-Post	1888–1889; 1894–1895	Hathi
Jülicher Kreis-, Correspondenz und Wochenblatt	1852–1864; 1866	UBONN

Title	Dates	Key
Juristische Zeitung für das Königreich Hannover	1828; 1837	GooBook
KAIN	1919	DHM
Kais. Königl. Schlesische Troppauer Zeitung	1816–1848	ANNO
Kaiserlich und kurpfalzbairische privilegirte allgemeine Zeitung	1806	GooBook
Kaiserlich-Königlich privilegirter Bothe von und für Tirol und Vorarlberg	1848	ALO
Kalender und Jahrbuch für Israeliten	1842–1851	CompMem
Kalender und Jahrbuch für Israeliten [II. Folge]	1854–1855	CompMem
Kalender und Jahrbuch für Israeliten [III. Folge]	1865–1868	CompMem
Kameralistische Zeitung	1836	GooBook
Kampfsignal	1932	DHM
Kanal-Zeitung	1888–1901; 1913–1918 articles	Dithm
Kartell-Convent Blätter	1910–1933	CompMem
Kartell-Mitteilungen	1924–1930	CompMem
Kaschauer Zeitung	1872–1914	DiFMOE
Kasselsches Journal	1847	Euro
Kattowitzer Zeitung	1930	SBC
Kattowitzer Zeitung	1875–1927 7 y; gaps	Euro
Kaufmännische Zeitschrift	1877–1904	NewsBank
Kaukasische Post	1906–1914	DiFMOE

Title	Dates	Key
Kemptner Zeitung	1841–1857; 1859–1873	Bavarica
Kikirikij	1861–1918	ANNO
Kirchenblatt für Sachsen-Weimar-Eisenach	1920	UJENA
Kirchlicher Anzeiger für Thüringen	1921	UJENA
Kirchlicher Gemeindeblatt für Reuss	1905–1919	UJENA
Kirchliches Amtsblatt für die Erzdiözesen Gnesen und Posen	1889	Poland
Kirchliches Verordnungsblatt für Sachsen-Weimar-Eisenach	1880–1921	UJENA
Kissinger Tagblatt	1870	GooBook
Kladderadatsch	1848–1944	UHEID
Kladderadatsch	1918 Nov 29	DHM
Klagenfurter Zeitung	1815–1875	ANNO
Kleine Presse	1914–1918	UFFM
Kolmarer Kreisblatt	1885–1887	ZEFYS
Kolmarer Kreiszeitung	1911; 1913; 1916–1918	ZEFYS
Kölnische Zeitung	1886 Aug	UHEID
Königlich Baierische Staats-Zeitung von München	1806	GooBook
Königlich baierisches Intelligenzblatt des Salzach-Kreises	1810	GooBook
Königlich baierisches Salzach-Blatt-Kreis	1811–1815	GooBook
Königlich bairisches Intelligenzblatt für den Regen-Kreis	1830–1837	GooBook

Title	Dates	Key
Königlich Bayerischer Polizey-Anzeiger für München	1820–1823	GooBook
Königlich bayerisches Amts- und Intelligenzblatt für die Pfalz	1838–1853	Bavarica
Königlich Bayerisches Intelligenzblatt für den Isar-Kreis	1825	GooBook
Königlich Bayerisches Intelligenz-Blatt für den Ober-Donau Kreis	1817–1837 (?)	GooBook
Königlich Bayerisches Intelligenzblatt für Mittelfranken	1839; 1854	GooBook
Königlich bayerisches Intelligenzblatt für Niederbayern	1838–1839	GooBook
Königlich bayerisches Intelligenz-Blatt für Oberfranken	1838–1852 10 y; gaps	GooBook
Königlich Bayerisches Kreis-Amts-Blatt der Oberpfalz und von Regensburg	1868	GooBook
Königlich Bayerisches Kreis-Amtsblatt für Oberbayern	1838	GooBook
Königlich Bayerisches Kreis-Amtsblatt von Unterfranken und Aschaffenburg	1873	GooBook
Königlich preußische Staats-Anzeiger	1868	GooBook
Königlich preußisches Central-Polizei-Blatt	1855; 1857–1865	GooBook
Königlich privilegirte Berlinische Zeitung von Staats- und gelehrten Sachen	1839; 1848–1849; 1857	ZEFYS
Königlich privilegirte Berlinische Zeitung von Staats- und gelehrten Sachen	1839–1919 8 y; many gaps	GooBook
Königlich Württembergisches Allgemeines Amts- und Intelligenz-Blatt für den Jaxt-Kreis	1826; 1831–1839	GooBook
Königlich-bayerisches Kreisamtsblatt der Pfalz	1854–1856	GooBook
Königlich-Bayerisches Kreis-Amtsblatt der Pfalz	1854–1872	Bavarica
Königlich-Bayerisches Kreis-Amtsblatt für Niederbayern	1854–1859	GooBook

Title	Dates	Key
Königliches Düsseldorfer Intelligenzblatt	1819–1820	UDUS
Königsberger allgemeine Zeitung	1942–1942	ZEFYS
Königsberger Hartungsche Zeitung	1886 Aug	UHEID
Kornblumen	1880	ZEFYS
Korrespondent für Deutschlands Buchdrucker und Schriftgießer	1870–1877; 1880–1897; 1900–1901	FES
Korrespondenzblatt des Vereins zur Gründung und Erhaltung einer Akademie für die Wissenschaft des Judentums	1920–1930	CompMem
Koschminer Zeitung und Anzeiger für die Städte Borek und Pogorzela	1909–1911; 1914	ZEFYS
Kösliner Volksblatt	1919	Euro
Kösliner Zeitung	1919; 1942	Euro
Kourier an der Donau: Zeitung für Niederbayern	1813–1847 9 y; gaps	GooBook
Krakauer Jüdische Zeitung	1898–1900	JDL
Kreis-Anzeiger für den Kresi Greifswald	1877–1895	UGRF
Kreis-Anzeiger von Landau	1816	Bavarica
Kreisblatt	1869–1870	UFULD
Kreisblatt des vorhinnigen Regierungsbezirkes Fulda	1866–1868	UFULD
Kreisblatt für den Kreis Malmedy	1866–1905	BelgArch
Kreisblatt für den Kreis Rees	1848	UBONN
Kreisblatt für den Neustädter Kreis	1845–1847	ZEFYS
Kreisblatt für die Kreisstadt Greifenhagen und Umgegend	1836	ZEFYS

Title	Dates	Key
Kreisblatt-Repertorium der Oberpfalz und von Regensburg	1872	GooBook
Kreis-Wochenblatt für den Kreis Adenau und Umgegend	1853–1854	UBONN
Kriegs-Zeitung	1915	Euro
Kriegszeitung der 7. Armee	1916–1918	UHEID
Kriegs-Zeitung der Elften Armee	1915–1916	BNF
Kriegs-Zeitung für das XV. Armee-Korps	1914–1916	BNF
Kritische Blätter der Börsen-Halle	1831	GooBook
Kroatischer Korrespondent	1789	CompMem
Kronstädter Zeitung	1848–1944	ANNO
Kunst und Volk	1924–1932	Poland
Kunstchronik	1866–1918	UHEID
Kurfürstlich gnäigst priviligirte Münchner Zeitung	1787	GooBook
Kurier für Niederbayern	1856–1873	GooBook
Kurier von der Mosel und den belgischen und französischen Gränzen	1792	DiLibri
Kyffhäuser	1936	DHM
La Tribune Juive (multilingual)	1923–1939	BNF
Lager-Echo	1916–1917	BritLib
Lähner Anzeiger	1908–1911; 1918–1919	ZEFYS
Laibacher Tagblatt	1868–1880	Slovenia

Title	Dates	Key
Laibacher Wochenblatt	1816; 1818; 1880–1893	Slovenia
Laibacher Zeitung	1784–1918	Slovenia
Landauer Wochenblatt	1823–1828	GooBook
Landesgesetzblatt für das Herzogtum Krain	1849–1914 47 y; gaps	Hathi
Landes-Gesetzblatt für das Königreich Böhmen	1848–1907 58 y; gaps	Hathi
Landes-Regierungsblatt für das Herzogthum Salzburg	1853	GooBook
Landes-Regierungsblatt für das Königreich Böhmen	1854–1857; 1859	Hathi
Landes-Zeitung für das Fürstenthum Reuß	1885–1902	UJENA
Landshuter Wochenblatt	1823–1828	GooBook
Landshuter Zeitung	1860; 1869; 1872–1873	GooBook
Landsturm	1915–1916	UHEID
Landsturm's Krieg's Bote	1914	BNF
Landwirthschaftliches Centralblatt	1853; 1855–1856; 1858–1859	GooBook
Landwirthschaftliches Wochenblatt für das Großherzogthum Baden	1833–1851 13 y; gaps	Hathi
Landwirthschaftliches Wochenblatt für Schleswig-Holstein	1891–1894	Hathi
Langensalzaer Kreis- und Nachrichtenblatt	1885–1902	UJENA
Langensalzaer Kreisblatt	1831–1911	UJENA
Langensalzaer Kreis-Wochenblatt	1824–1830	UJENA
Langensalzaer Tageblatt	1911–1916	UJENA

Title	Dates	Key
Langensalzaer Wochenblatt	1701–1818	UJENA
Langensalzaisches Wochenblat	1760–1798	UJENA
Lappland-Kurier	1945	DHM
Lausizisches Wochenblatt	1790–1792	UBIEL
Lauterbacher Anzeiger	1859–1860	UDARM
Le Juif (bilingual)	1923	BNF
Leipziger Intelligenz-Blatt	1765	ArchOrg
Leipziger Intelligenz-Blatt	1760–1804	GooBook
Leipziger Intelligenz-Blatt	1766–1807 19 y; gaps	Hathi
Leipziger Lokomotive	1843 Feb 1	Lpzg
Leipziger Mieter-Zeitung	1923	DHM
Leipziger Neueste Nachrichten	1935	DHM
Leipziger Tageblatt	1812–1813	Hathi
Leipziger Tageblatt und Anzeiger	1886 Aug	UHEID
Leipziger Tageszeitung	1933	DHM
Leipziger Uhrmacher-Zeitung	1900	UDRES
Leipziger Völkisches-Echo	1924 Nov 22	DHM
Leipziger Volkszeitung	1927	DHM
Leipziger Zeitungen	1739–1746; 1748	ZEFYS

Title	Dates	Key
Leipzig's roter Straßenbahner	1933	DHM
Lemberger Zeitung	1812–1866	ANNO
Liberales Judentum	1908–1922	CompMem
Liechtensteiner Heimatdienst	1933–1935	Liecht
Liechtensteiner Landeszeitung	1863–1867	Liecht
Liechtensteiner Nachrichten	1924–1935	Liecht
Liechtensteiner Vaterland	1936–2005	Liecht
Liechtensteiner Volkblatt	1878–2005	Liecht
Liechtensteiniche Wochenzeitung	1873–1877	Liecht
Lienzer Zeitung	1868–1915; 1919; 1938–1945	Tessmann
Liller Kriegszeitung	1914–1918	UHEID
Lindauer Tagblatt für Stadt und Land	1870–1873	GooBook
Linnaea	1826–1882	Bio
Linzer Tagespost	1865–1943	ANNO
Linzer Volksblatt	1870–1875	Euro
Linzer Volksblatt	1870–1938	ANNO
Linzer Zeitung	1844	GooBook
Lippische Intelligenzblätter	1767–1808	NRW Lib
Lippische Landes-Zeitung	1886 Aug	UHEID

Title	Dates	Key
Lippisches Intelligenzblatt	1809–1842	NRW Lib
Lippisches Volksblatt	1848–1852	Lippe
Literarisches Centralblatt für Deutschland	1850–1919	GooBook
Maiser Wochenblatt	1903–1915	Tessmann
Mallersdorfer Anzeiger	1902–1926 (coming)	BavLib
Malmedy-St. Vither Volkszeitung	1905–1934	BelgArch
Mannheimer Intelligenzblatt	1790–1792	GooBook
Marburger Zeitung	1860; 1872; 1882–1891; 1893–1918	ANNO
Marburger Zeitung	1866–1945 76 y; gaps	DiFMOE
Mayener Volkszeitung	1876–1919 29 y; gaps	UBONN
Mecklenburgische gemeinnützige Blätter	1790–1793	UBIEL
Mecklenburgische Anzeigen	1886 Aug	UHEID
Medicinisch-chirurgische Zeitung	1815	GooBook
Medizinische Zeitung	1852–1853	Hathi
Medizinisches Wochenblatt	1783–1789; 1792–1793	UGOT
Meininger Tageblatt	1849–1956 (coming)	UJENA
Meldereiter im Sundgau	1915–1918	UHEID
Memminger Bezirksamtsblatt	1863–1869	GooBook
Menorah	1923–1932	CompMem

Title	Dates	Key
Meraner Zeitung	1855–1926 59 y; gaps	Tessmann
Metallarbeiter Jugend	1920–1932 6 y; gaps	FES
Milchwirtschaftliches Zentralblatt	1887	GooBook
Militär-Wochenblatt	1816–1919 92 y; gaps	Hathi
Militär-Zeitung	1857–1868	GooBook
Militär-Zeitung	1872–1896 19 y; gaps	Hathi
Miltenberger Tagblatt	1863–1865	GooBook
Minnesota Staats-Zeitung	1858–1872	Chron
Mitausche Zeitung	1905–1906	Latvia
Mitteilungen aus dem Verband der Vereine für jüdische Geschichte und Literatur in Deutschland	1895–1921	CompMem
Mitteilungen der Arbeitsgemeinschaft jüdisch-liberale Jugendvereine Deutschlands	1919–1922	CompMem
Mitteilungen der Gesellschaft für jüdische Volkskunde [Alte Folge]	1898–1904	CompMem
Mitteilungen der Gesellschaft für jüdische Volkskunde [Neue Folge]	1905–1929	CompMem
Mitteilungen des Gesamtarchivs der deutschen Juden	1909–1914: 1926	CompMem
Mitteilungsblatt der Arbeitsgemeinschaft freier Angestelltenverbände	1919–1920	FES
Mitteilungsblatt des Ortskommittes der RGO Leipzig	1933 Feb 12	DHM
Mittelbayerische Zeitung	1945–1950	DigiPress
Mitteldeutsche Rundschau	1914–1918	UFFM

Title	Dates	Key
Mittelrheinische Landeszeitung	1935–1939	UBONN
Mittelrheinische Sportzeitung	1920–1925	UDARM
Mittheilungen aus Oldenburg	1835–1848	UOLD
Mohácser Wochenblatt	1879–1880	OSZK
Molkerei-Zeitung	1887–1913 9 y; gaps	GooBook
Möllers deutsche Gärtner-Zeitung	1886; 1895; 1897	GooBook
Monatsschrift für Geschichte und Wissenschaft des Judentums	1851–1939	CompMem
Montagspost	1940	DHM
Montags-Zeitung	1898–1922	ANNO
Montjoiér Volksblatt	1880–1936	UKLN
Morgenblatt für gebildete Stände	1816–1849	UHEID
Morgenpost	1854–1859; 1869–1886	BavLib
Moskauer Rundschau	1932 Jul 24	DHM
Mülhauer Frauenzeitung	1901–1929 19 y; gaps	BNF
Mülhauser Tagblatt	1914–1918; 1944	BNF
Münchener Amtsblatt	1793–18??	Bavarica
Münchener Conversations-Blatt	1831–1832; 1844	GooBook
Münchener Guckkasten	1888–1891	DigiPress
Münchener Herold	1851–1853	GooBook

Title	Dates	Key
Münchener Omnibus	1862	GooBook
Münchener Post	1930; 1932–1933	DHM
Münchener Ratsch-Kathl	1889–1907	DigiPress
Münchener Stadtanzeiger und Münchener Ratsch-Kathl	1908–1914	DigiPress
Münchener Wochenblatt für das katholische Volk	1868–1869	DigiPress
Münchener Zeitung	1848	Euro
Münchner Intelligenzblatt	1779; 1789	GooBook
Münchner Staats-, gelehrte und vermischte Nachrichten	1782	GooBook
Münchner Zeitung	1786	GooBook
Münsterberger Kreisblatt	1888–1931 17 y; gaps	ZEFYS
Münsterberger Wochenblatt	1840–1848	ZEFYS
Münsterische Universitäts-Zeitung	1907–1914	UMST
Münsterisches gemeinnütziges Wochenblatt	1785–1803	UMST
Münsterisches Intelligenzblatt	1765–1849	UMST
Musikalische Real-Zeitung	1789	GooBook
Musikalisches Wochenblatt	1892–1910	UJENA
Muskauer Wochenblatt	1821–1822, 1824	ZEFYS
Nachalath Zewi	1930–1938	CompMem
Nachrichtendienst	1922–1928	CompMem

Title	Dates	Key
Nationalzeitung	1906–1907	CompMem
National-Zeitung	1857–1857	ZEFYS
National-Zeitung	1886 Aug	UHEID
Naturwissenschaftliche Rundschau	1887–1912	Bio
Naumburger Briefe	1919 Apr 20	DHM
Naumburger Kreisblatt	1845	GooBook
Naumburger Tageblatt	1911	UHAL
Neckar-Zeitung	1822–1823; 1825–1828	GooBook
Neu Braunfelser Zeitung	1852–1853	TX Hist
Neu-ankommender Currier Auß Wienn	1622–1639	UBREM
Neubau und Siedlung	1931	DHM
Neuburger Wochenblatt	1862–1863; 1866–1868; 1871–1873	GooBook
Neue Allgemeine Wiener Handlungs- und Industrie-Zeitung	1827–1828	ANNO
Neue Aschaffenburger Zeitung und Aschaffenburger Anzeiger	1865–1866	GooBook
Neue Augsburger Zeitung	1830	GooBook
Neue Bonner Zeitung	1796–1895 8 y; major gaps	UBONN
Neue Breslauer Zeitung	1821	GooBook
Neue Didaskalia	1856–1873	GooBook

Title	Dates	Key
Neue Folge der Gesundheits-Zeitung	1840–1850	ANNO
Neue Fränkische Zeitung	1848–1850	DigiPress
Neue Freie Presse	1864–1939	ANNO
Neue Hamburger Zeitung	1896–1922	Euro
Neue jenaische allgemeine Literatur-Zeitung	1842–1848	UJENA
Neue jüdische Monatshefte	1916–1920	CompMem
Neue kielische gelehrte Zeitung	1797	UKIEL
Neue Kino Rundschau	1917–1921	ANNO
Neue Leipziger Zeitung	1940–1941	DHM
Neue Lodzer Zeitung	1908 Jul–Dec	DiFMOE
Neue Mannigfaltigkeiten	1774–1777	UBIEL
Neue Militär-Zeitung	1856–1858; 1859–1860	GooBook
Neue Mülhauser Zeitung	1914–1918	BNF
Neue Nationalzeitung	1907–1916	CompMem
Neue Nürnbergische gelehrte Zeitung	1791	GooBook
Neue Post	1918–1919	DiFMOE
Neue Preußische Zeitung	1848 Sep 23	DHM
Neue preußische Zeitung	1857–1859, 1867–1868	ZEFYS
Neue preußische Zeitung	1886 Aug	UHEID

Title	Dates	Key
Neue Rheinische Zeitung	1953	Euro
Neue Speyerer Zeitung	1817–1853 30 y; gaps	Bavarica
Neue Vetchauer Zeitung	1902–1944 12 y; many gaps	ZEFYS
Neue Warte am Inn	1881–1943	ANNO
Neue wöchentliche Rostock'sche Nachrichten und Anzeigen	1842 Feb 17	WikiS
Neue Würzburger Zeitung	1842–1872 10 y; gaps	GooBook
Neue Zeit	1945–1994 (special login)	ZEFYS
Neue Zeitung	1906–1907	CompMem
Neue Zeitungen von gelehrten Sachen	1715–1770; 1773–1774; 1776–1784	UJENA
Neue Zürcher Zeitung	1780–present	NZZ
Neue Zürcher Zeitung	1886 Aug	UHEID
Neuer Anzeiger	1885	UDARM
Neuer Bayerischer Kurier für Stadt und Land	1864–1868	GooBook
Neuer Rheinischer Merkur	1819	GooBook
Neuer Rheinischer Merkur	1817–1818	UJENA
Neues 8–Uhr Blatt	1914–1925	ANNO
Neues Budapester Abendblatt	1919	DiFMOE
Neues Deutschland	1946–1990 (special login)	ZEFYS
Neues Fremdenblatt	1865–1876	ANNO

Title	Dates	Key
Neues Journal für die Botanik	1806–1810	Bio
Neues Münchener Tagblatt	1848–1849	DigiPress
Neues St. Petersburgisches Journal	1783–1784	GooBook
Neues Tagblatt aus der östlichen Schweiz	1856–1873	Switz
Neues Tagblatt für München und Bayern	1839	GooBook
Neues Volksblatt	1851	GooBook
Neues Wiener Journal	1911	ANNO
Neues Wiener Tagblatt	1900–1905; 1930–1931	ANNO
Neueste Mittheilungen	1882–1892	ZEFYS
Neueste preußische Zeitung	1849	UFFM
Neueste Weltbegebenheiten	1823–1831 1833–1840	Bavarica
Neueste Zeitung	1831–1842	UFFM
Neuigkeiten	1912–1916	OK Hist
Neulengbacher Zeitung (Wienerwald-Bote)	1900–1943	ANNO
Neustädter Kreisblatt	1832–1844; 1846–1848	GooBook
Neustädter Kreisblatt	1852–1911 27 y; gaps	ZEFYS
Neustädter Kreisbote	1818–1854	UJENA
Neustettiner Kreisblatt	1862–1869	ZEFYS
Neustrelitzer Zeitung	1886 Aug	UHEID

Title	Dates	Key
Neuwieder Intelligenz- und Kreis-Blatt	1849–1855	UBONN
Neuwiedische Nachrichten	1846–1855	UBONN
New Orleanser Deutsche Zeitung	1876–1906	GooNews
Newe Zeitung	1857	UBREM
Newe Zeitung und eigentlicher Bericht . . .	1620	DiLibri
Niederösterreichischer Grenzbote	1912–1918; 1920–1943	ANNO
Niederrheinische Musik-Zeitung für Kunstfreunde und Künstler	1853	GooBook
Niederrheinischer Kurier	1831	GooBook
Nordböhmisches Volksblatt	1873; 1883	ANNO
Norddeutsche allgemeine Zeitung	1884	CRL
Norddeutsche Allgemeine Zeitung	1886 Aug	UHEID
Norddeutsche Nachrichten (coming)	1879–1943	Euro
Nordenburger Anzeiger	1876	ARCOR
Nördlinger Wochenblatt	1849–1850	GooBook
Nördlingisches Intelligenz- und Wochenblatt	1811–1814	GooBook
Nördlingsche wöchentliche Nachrichten	1766–1768	Bavarica
Nordmährische Rundschau	1913–1919	ANNO
Nordwestliche Post	1818 Nov 13–1822 Jul 26	NewsBank
Northumberland Republikaner	1812 Aug 12–1818 Jan 2	NewsBank

Title	Dates	Key
Notariatsblatt für das Großherzogthum Baden	1852–1870	ZEFYS
Notariats-Blatt für das Großherzogthum Baden	1852–1870	Hathi
Notiz-Blatt des Architekten- und Ingenieur-Verein für das Königreich Hannover	1853	GooBook
Numismatische Zeitung	1842	GooBook
Nürnberger Abendblatt	1844–1845	GooBook
Nürnberger Stadtzeitung	1873	GooBook
Nürnberger Tagblatt	1848–1850	DigiPress
Oberdeutsche Staatszeitung	1787	GooBook
Oberelsässische Landes-Zeitung	1815; 1914–1918	BNF
Ober-Elsäßischer Volksfreund: Anzeiger für Hüningen, Sierenz und die angrenzenden Kantone	1914–1918	BNF
Oberhessische Volkszeitung	1911–1916	UDARM
Oberlausitzische Fama	1824–1827; 1831	ZEFYS
Oberrheinische Nachrichten	1914–1924	Liecht
Oberschlesisches Wochenblatt	1920	SilDIg
Octoberfest-Zeitung	1905	BavLib
Oedenburger Arbeiterrat	1919	DiFMOE
Oedenburger Proletariat	1919 Jul-Aug	DiFMOE
Oedenburger Zeitung	1888–1919 25 y; gaps	DiFMOE

Title	Dates	Key
Oesterreichische Jugend-Zeitschrift	1849; 1851	ANNO
Oesterreichisches Bürgerblatt	1831	GooBook
Oettingisches Wochenblatt	1788–1823 31 y; gaps	Bavarica
Offenbacher Abendblatt	1914	UDARM
Offenbacher Zeitung	1912	UDARM
Öffentlicher Anzeiger der königlich preussischen Regierung zu Cleve	1816–1821	UDUS
Öffentlicher Anzeiger der königlichen Regierung zu Posen	1818; 1827	Posen
Öffentlicher Anzeiger: Amtsblatt für den Stadtkreis Frankfurt a. M.	1914–1918	UFFM
Officielle Beilage für amtliche Bekanntmachungen	1863	Hathi
Oklahoma Neuigkeiten	1912–1916	OK Hist
Oppositions-Blatt oder Weimarische Zeitung	1816–1820	GooBook
Ordentliche wöchentliche Franckfurter Frag- und Anzeigungs-Nachrichten	1750–1864 66 y; major gaps	GooBook
Ordinari Sontags-Zeitung, aus Deutschland, Polen Schweden	1657	UBREM
Ordinari-Münchner-Zeitungen	1760	GooBook
Organe Malmedy	1893–1901	UBONN
Osnabrücker Zeitung	1919 Jun 1	Euro
Ost und West	1901–1923	CompMem
Österreichische Buchhändler-Korrespondenz	1860–1875	Euro
Österreichische Illustrirte Zeitung	1894–1938	ANNO

Title	Dates	Key
Österreichische Land-Zeitung	1903–1918	ANNO
Österreichische Lehrerinnen-Zeitung	1893–1901	ANNO
Österreichische Nähmaschinen- und Fahrrad-Zeitung	1904–1938	ANNO
Österreichische Volkszeitung	1907	ANNO
Österreichischer Beobachter	1810–1847 27 y; gaps	Hathi
Österreichisches entomologisches Wochenblatt	1851–1857	Bio
Österreichisches pädagogisches Wochenblatt	1842–1865	Euro
Österreichisch-ungarisches Cantoren-Zeitung	1881–1897	CompMem
Osthavelländisches Kreisblatt	1849–1859; 1890–1892	ZEFYS
Ostholsteinischer Anzeiger	1802–2006 (needs login)	Eutin
Ostpreußische Zeitung	1886 Aug	UHEID
Ostsee-Zeitung	1886 Aug	UHEID
Paderbornschezirks Intelligenzblatt für den Appellationsgerichts-Bezirk	1820–1843 11 y; gaps	GooBook
Palästina	1902–1938	CompMem
Palästina Nachrichten	1934–1936	CompMem
Palatina	1859–1862; 1869–1873	GooBook
Pannonia	1837–1848	DiFMOE
Passauer Neue Presse	1946–1965	DigiPress
Passauer Tagblatt	1873	GooBook

Title	Dates	Key
Passavia	1829; 1840–1843; 1845–1846	GooBook
Pastoralblatt	1870–1908	Hathi
Pennsylvanischer Staatsbote	1776 Jul 4	Germpuls
Permanente Revolution	1932	DHM
Pester Lloyd	1888; 1891–1922	ANNO
Pester Lloyd	1908–1910	ANLib
Pesther Tageblatt	1841	GooBook
Pettauer Zeitung	1890–1904	Slovenia
Pfälzer Demokrat und Sonntags-Blatt	1870–1871	GooBook
Pfälzer Sonntagsblatt	1867–1869	GooBook
Pfälzer Unterhaltungsblatt	1865–1866	GooBook
Pfälzer Zeitung	1850–1858	Bavarica
Pfälzer-Bote für das Glantal und Anzeige-Blatt für den Bezirk Kusel	1857–1873	Bavarica
Pfälzische Blätter	1853–1873	Bavarica
Pfälzische Post	1871; 1873	GooBook
Pfälzische Volkszeitung	1865–1871	GooBook
Pfälzischer Kurier	1865–1868; 1870–1871; 1873	Bavarica
Pfälzischer Zeitung	1859–1872	Bavarica
Pfälzisches Sonntags-Blatt	1867–1869	GooBook

Title	Dates	Key
Pfalz-Neuburgische Provinzialblätter	1803; 1805–1806; 1808	GooBook
Philadelphischer Wochenblat	1790–?	Newspapers
Philanthropin	1869–1915	CompMem
Pilsner Tagblatt	1900–1918	ANNO
Pittsburger Volksblatt	1859–1900	GooNews
Plauderstübchen	1848; 1850–1851; 1866–1868	GooBook
Pola	1883–1885	UPULA
Polaer Tagblatt	1905–1918	UPULA
Politische Frauen-Zeitung	1869–1871	ANNO
Politische Zeitung im Saar-Departement	1798–1799	DiLibri
Politischer Gevattersmann	1848	DigiPress
Polizei-Blatt für das Herzogthum Salzburg	1872	GooBook
Polyhymnia	1832–1833	Bavarica
Pommersche Zeitung	1860	Euro
Pommersche Zeitung	1875–1937 8 y; gaps	CRL
Pommersche Zeitung	1935, 1937–1939	ZEFYS
Pommersche-Zeitung	1886 Aug	UHEID
Populäre österreichische Gesundheits-Zeitung	1830–1840	ANNO

Title	Dates	Key
Populär-wissenschaftliche Monatsblätter zur Belehrung über das Judentum für Gebildete aller Confessionen	1881–1908	CompMem
Posener-Zeitung	1886 Aug	UHEID
PostZeitung	1636	UBREM
Prager Abendblatt	1872–1875	ANNO
Preßburger Zeitung	1766–1898 130 y; gaps	DiFMOE
Preßburgisches Wochenblatt	1771–1773	DiFMOE
Pressedienst des Generalgouvernements	1940–1943	ZEFYS
Preußische Provinzial-Blätter	1834–1860 9 y; gaps	GooBook
Preußische Zeitung	1944–1944	ZEFYS
Prossnitzer Wochenblatt	1871–1875	Kram
Protestantische Kirchenzeitung	1886 Aug	UHEID
Provinzialblatt	1848–1849	GateBay
Provinzial-Blatt für das Großherzogthum Fulda	1815–1821	UFULD
Provinzial-Correspondenz	1863–1884	ZEFYS
Punch	1849–1850	GooBook
Pustertaler Bote	1850–1927	Tessmann
Ragniter Kreisblatt	1882–1883; 1885–1886	ZEFYS
Raketen	1881	DiLibri

Title	Dates	Key
Reading Adler	1796 Jan 3–1825 Dec 27	NewsBank
Regensburger Anzeiger	1867	GooBook
Regensburger Conversations-Blatt	1840–1842	GooBook
Regensburger Intelligenzblatt	1810–1812; 1814	GooBook
Regensburger Morgenblatt	1861–1867; 1869–1872	GooBook
Regensburger Neueste Nachrichten	1911–1925 (coming)	BavLib
Regensburger Wochenblatt	1837; 1870	GooBook
Regensburger Zeitung	1843; 1854–1855; 1858–1859	GooBook
Regierungs- und Gesetzblatt für das Königreich Bayern	1819	GooBook
Regierungs- und Gesetzblatt für das Königreich Bayern	1821–1825	Hathi
Regierungs- und Intelligenzblatt für das Herzogtum Coburg	1840–1964	DigiPress
Regierungs- und Nachrichtenblatt für Sachsen-Weimar-Eisenach	1919–1921	UJENA
Regierungsblatt der Militär-Regierung Württemberg-Baden	1946–1952	Baden
Regierungsblatt für das Großherzogthum Sachsen-Weimar-Eisenach	1893–1912	Hathi
Regierungs-Blatt für das Großherzogthum Sachsen-Weimar-Eisenach	1817–1820; 1822–1823	Hathi
Regierungs-Blatt für das Herzogtum Coburg	1865–1918	DigiPress
Regierungsblatt für das Königreich Bayern	1826–1872	Hathi
Regierungsblatt für das Königreich Württemberg	1806–1922 81 y; gaps	Hathi
Regierungsblatt für das Land Thüringen	1945–1949	UJENA

Title	Dates	Key
Regierungsblatt für das Markgrafthum Mähren	1855–1859	GooBook
Regierungsblatt für Mecklenburg	1842–1922 48 y; gaps (*–1930)	Hathi
Regierungsblatt für Mecklenburg-Schwerin Amtliche Beilage	1873–1919 27 y; gaps	Hathi
Regierungsblatt für Sachsen-Weimar-Eisenach	1837–1844	UJENA
Regierungsblatt für Thüringen	1952	UJENA
Regierungsblatt für Württemberg	1920–1922 (*–1927)	Hathi
Reichs-Gesetz-Blatt für das Kaiserthum Österreich	1854–1864; 1866	GooBook
Reichspost	1894–1938	ANNO
Reichswart	1920–1936	ZEFYS
Relation aller Fuernemmen und gedenckwuerdigen Historien	1609	UHEID
Rendsburger Tagespost	coming	Rndsbg
Resolution, Welche etliche Obristen, mit dem Fürsten von Friedland . . .	1634	UBREM
Revalsche Post-Zeitung	1709 Oct 18	Est
Rhein- und Mosel-Bote	1853–1855	UBONN
Rhein- und Nahe-Zeitung	1910–1941	UDARM
Rheinbacher Anzeige	1910	UBONN
Rheinbacher Kreisblatt	1850–1864	UBONN
Rheinbayerisches Volksblatt	1836	GooBook
Rheinhessischer Beobachter	1856–1873	UDARM

Title	Dates	Key
Rheinisch Westfälische Zeitung	1886 Aug	UHEID
Rheinisch-Bergische Zeitung	1830–1945	UBONN
Rheinische Allgemeine Zeitung	1840–1842	UKLN
Rheinische Allgemeine Zeitung	1869–1870	UBONN
Rheinische Blätter	1816–1820	GooBook
Rheinischer Humorist	1860	DiLibri
Rheinischer Merkur	1814–1816	UDUS
Rheinisches conservatives Volksblatt	1865	UBONN
Rheinisches Land	1926–1928	FES
Rheinisches Wochenblatt	1838	UBONN
Rheinisches Wochenblatt für Stadt und Land	1834–1837	UBONN
Rheinsberger Zeitung	1912; 1922; 1925–1942	ZEFYS
Rheinsberger Zeitung: Illustrirte Unterhaltungsbeilage	1925–1926	ZEFYS
Rhön-Zeitung	1892–1941 41 y; gaps	UJENA
Rieder Intelligenzblatt	1810	GooBook
Rigaische Rundschau	1908–1920	Euro
Rigasche Zeitung	1869–1918	Latvia
Rigische Novellen	1681–1699	UBREM
Rohö Zeitung	1921 Feb	Euro

Title	Dates	Key
Rosenheimer Anzeiger	1864–1925 59 y; gaps	BavLib
Rosenheimer Tagblatt Wendelstein	1877–1912 22 y; gaps	BavLib
Rosenheimer Wochenblatt	1833–1834; 1855–1863	BavLib
Rostocker Zeitung	1886 Aug	UHEID
Rummelsburger Zeitung	1930	Euro
Rundschau der Frau	1930–1933	FES
Rundschreiben des Präfekten von Bozen	1944–1945	Tessmann
Rybniker Kreisblatt	1842–1846; 1919	ZEFYS
Saar- und Mosel-Zeitung	1886 Aug	UHEID
Sachsenpost	1934	DHM
Sachsenzeitung	1830–1834	Dres
Salzburger Chronik	1873–1918	ANNO
Salzburger Intelligenzblatt	1794–1810 15 y; gaps	GooBook
Salzburger Volksblatt	1881	ANNO
Salzburger Wacht	1914	ANNO
Sammlung der Administrativ-Verordnungen und Bekanntmachungen für den Oberrhein-Kreis	1837–1838	GooBook
San Antonio Zeitung	1854 Jul 14	TX Hist
Sanct-Paulinus-Blatt für das deutsche Volk	1875	DiLibri

Title	Dates	Key
Sangerhäuser Kreisblatt	1855–1857	UHAL
Sankt Pöltener Diözesanblatt	1914–1939 19 y; gaps	ANNO
Sattler- und Portefeuiller Zeitung	1909–1915	FES
Sattler- und Tapezierer Zeitung	1899–1900	FES
Sattler-Tapezierer- und Portefeuiller Zeitung	1923–1933	FES
Sattler-Zeitung	1900–1902; 1908	FES
Schaffhauser Nachrichen	1861–2014	Schaffhsn
Schild und Schwert	1848	GooBook
Schlesische Landarbeiter	1919–1922	Poland
Schlesische Priviligirte Staats-, Kriegs- und Friedens-Zeitung	1742–1779 16 y; gaps	Poland
Schlesische Provinzialblätter	1862; 1864–1867	Hathi
Schlesische Zeitung	1813 Mar 3	Raether
Schlesische Zeitung	1886 Aug	UHEID
Schlesisches Pastoralblatt	1880–1929	Poland
Schlesisische Arbeiterzeitung	1919–1926	FES
Schleswig-Holsteinische Blätter	1835–1840	GooBook
Schleswig-Holsteinische Provinzialblätter	1787–1798	UBIEL
Schleswig-Holsteinische Tageszeitung	coming	Rndsbg
Schlettstadter Tageblatt	1914–1918	BNF

Title	Dates	Key
Schneider-Zeitung	1904–1920	FES
Schrattenthals Frauenzeitung	1893–1894	DiFMOE
Schützengrabenzeitung	1915–1916	UHEID
Schwäbischer Merkur	1801–1872 12 y; gaps	GooBook
Schwarzburger Bote	1926–1934	UJENA
Schwedter Tageblatt	1925–1941 14 y; gaps	ZEFYS
Schweinfurter Tagblatt	1863; 1865–1873; 1875	GooBook
Schweinfurter Tagblatt	1863–1873	BavLib
Schweizer Schule	1893–2000 coming	e-lib.ch
Schweizerische Bienen-Zeitung	1898	GooBook
Schweizerische Tagblätter	1798	Switz
Scranton Wochenblatt	1869–1918	Chron
Sechseläuten Tagblatt	1851	GooBook
Seelower Tageblatt	1943–1943	ZEFYS
Seille-Bote	1915–1916	BNF
Selbst-Emancipation	1885–1893	CompMem
Shanghai Echo	1947	DNB
Sichel und Hammer	1925	DHM
Sickinger Bote	1862–1863	Bavarica

Title	Dates	Key
Siebenbürger Bote	1842–1848	DiFMOE
Siebenbürger Wochenblatt	1861	GooBook
Siebenbürgisch-Deutsches Tageblatt	1874–1941 34 y; gaps	DiFMOE
Siebenbürgisch-Deutsches Tageblatt	1886 Aug	UHEID
Siebenbürgische Provinzialblätter	1808	GooBook
Siebenbürgische Zeitung	1950–present	SbgZ
Siebenbürgisches Bürgerblatt	1838–1839	GooBook
Siebenbürgisches Wochenblatt	1869–1870	Hathi
Siegburger Kreisblatt	1862–1866	UBONN
Simplicissimus	1896–1944	Simplic
Sinai	1846	Hathi
Sinziger Volksfreund	1894	DiLibri
Sobernheim-Kirner Intelligenz-Blatt	1864–1867	UBONN
Social-politische Frauen-Zeitung	1875–1876	ANNO
Solidarität	1900–1924	FES
Solinger Kreis-Intelligenzblatt	1857–1868	UBONN
Solothurnisches Wochenblatt	1810–1834	Hathi
Sonnstagsblatt	1787	GooBook
Sonntagsblatt	1914	UFFM

Title	Dates	Key
Sonntagsblatt	1831–1849; 1851–1853	Bavarica
Sonntagsgruss unserer Heimatkirche	1928–1930	UJENA
Sonntagsgruß: Kirchlicher Anzeiger für Frankfurt a.M. und Umgebung	1914	UFFM
Sonntagsgruß: Reußisches Kirchenblatt für Stadt und Land	1925–1928	UJENA
Sonntagspost	1914	CRL
Sorauer Kreisblatt	1843–1847	ZEFYS
Sorauer Tageblatt	1923–1944 15 y; gaps	ZEFYS
Sorauer Wochenblatt für Unterhaltung, Belehrung und Ereignisse der Gegenwart	1817–1846 9 y; gaps	ZEFYS
Sozialistische Arbeiter-Zeitung	1931–1933	FES
Spandauer Zeitung	1925; 1931; 1933	ZEFYS
Spartacus	1849	UBONN
Spartakus	1929	DHM
Speyerer Tagblatt	1870	GooBook
Speyerer wöchentliches Anzeige-Blatt	1823; 1825; 1828	GooBook
Sprottauer Wochenzeitung	1839–1840; 1845–1846	ZEFYS
St. Galler Volksblatt	1856–1900	Switz
St. Galler Zeitung	1831–1881	Switz
St. Goarer Kreisblatt	1839–1850	UBONN
St. Vither Volkszeitung	1834–1941; 1955–1964	BelgArch

Title	Dates	Key
Staats- und Gelehrte-Zeitung des unpartheyischen Correspondenten	1731; 1795; 1814	Hathi
Staats- und Gelehrte-Zeitung des unpartheyischen Correspondenten	1795–1826	Gale
Staats- und Gelehrte-Zeitung des unpartheyischen Correspondenten	1806–1812	Hathi
Staats- und Regierungsblatt für Baiern	1806–1817	Hathi
Staats- und Regierungsblatt für Hamburg	1890–1920	Hathi
Staats-Anzeiger für das Grossherzogtum Baden	1869–1873; 1908	Hathi
Stadt- und Landbote	1867–1936	UKLN
Stadt- und Wochenblatt	1848–1849	ZEFYS
Stenographische Protokolle der Verhandlungen der Zionisten-Kongresse	1897–1937 19 y; gaps	CompMem
Sterzinger Bezirks-Anzeiger	1907–1908	Tessmann
Stettiner Entomologische Zeitung	1912	Bio
Stettiner General-Anzeiger	1936–1937	ZEFYS
Stettiner Zeitung	1886 Aug	UHEID
Steyermärkische Intelligenz-Blätter der Grätzer Zeitung	1824	GooBook
Stimme der Kirche	1871–1876	UJENA
Stobsiade: Stobser Zeitung	1914	Swarth
Stolper Neueste Nachrichten	1901–1918	Euro
Stolper Wochenblatt	1858	Koszalin
Strassburger Bürger-Zeitung	1616; 1892–1893; 1914–1918	BNF

Title	Dates	Key
Strassburger Diözesanblatt	1899; 1914–1918	BNF
Straßburger Handelsblatt	1873	GooBook
Strassburger neueste Nachrichten: General-Anzeiger für Strassburg und Elsass-Lothringen	1914–1918	BNF
Strassburger Post	1914–1918	BNF
Strassburger priveligierte Zeitung	1788–1791; 1793–1794	BNF
Strassburgisches Wochenblatt (bilingual)	1788–1789	BNF
Straubinger Tagblatt	1861–1875	GooBook
Strehlener Stadtblatt	1835–1843	ZEFYS
Süd Australische Zeitung	1860–1874	Trove
Südaustralische Zeitung	1850–1851	Trove
Südböhmische Volkszeitung	1936–1938	DiFMOE
Süddeutsche Blätter für Leben, Wissenschaft und Kunst	1831; 1837–1838; 1841–1845	GooBook
Süddeutscher Anzeiger	1863–1865	GooBook
Süddeutscher Geschäftsanzeiger	1864–1865	GooBook
Sudetendeutsche Zeitung	1951–1955	DigiPress
Sudetenland	1951	BavLib
Südösterreichische Nachrichten	1910	UPULA
Südsteirische Post	1881	ANNO

Title	Dates	Key
Südtiroler Heimat	1923–1938	Tessmann
Südtiroler Landeszeitung	1920–1922	Tessmann
Südtiroler Nachrichten	1963–1974	Tessmann
Südtiroler Ruf	1956–1984	Tessmann
Südtiroler Volksblatt	1862–1925	Tessmann
Suhler Zeitung	1919–1931	UJENA
Sulamith	1806–1848 37 y; gaps	CompMem
Sulzbacher Wochenblatt	1870–1871	GooBook
Sundine	1840	GooBook
Tag-Blatt der Stadt Bamberg	1834	OPACPlus
Tagblatt für die Kreishauptstadt Augsburg	1830	GooBook
Tagblatt für die Städte Dillingen, Lauingen, Höchstadt, Wertingen und Gundelfingen	1856	GooBook
Tagblatt für Landshut und Umgegend	1848	GooBook
Tägliche Rundschau	1886 Aug	UHEID
Täglicher Anzeiger für Berg und Mark	1850–1868; 1872–1873	UBONN
Tags-Blatt für München	1827	GooBook
Teltower Kreisblatt	1856–1896	ZEFYS
Teplitz-Schönauer Anzeiger	1861–1919	ANNO
Teschner Zeitung	1919–1932 10 y; gaps	Cieszyn

Title	Dates	Key
Teutsches Volksblatt	1848–1849	DigiPress
Theater-Zeitung	1846	UMST
Theatralisches Wochenblatt	1802	UMST
Thorner Freiheit	1939–1945	Poland
Thorner Wochenblatt	1816–1868	Poland
Thorner Zeitung	1796–1842 17 y; gaps	Euro
Thüringer Kirchenblatt	1849–1851	UJENA
Thüringer Kirchenblatt und Kirchlicher Anzeiger	1922–1943; 1945–1947; 1949	UJENA
Thüringer Kirchenblatt: Gesetz- und Verordnungsblatt	1920–1921	UJENA
Thüringer Lehrerzeitung	1912–1921	UJENA
Thüringer Volk	1950	UJENA
Thüringer Volksfreund	1829–1831	UJENA
Tilsiter allgemeine Zeitung	1914; 1916–1917	ZEFYS
Tilsiter Zeitung	1894, 1914	ZEFYS
Tiroler Volksbote	1892–1919	Tessmann
Tiroler Zeitung	1850–1853	Tessmann
Traun-Alz Bote	1869–1872	GooBook
Traun-Alz-Salzach Bote	1873	GooBook
Treffurter Wochenblatt	1849	ZEFYS

Title	Dates	Key
Treviris	1834–1836	GooBook
Tribunal	1932	DHM
Trierische Staats- und gelehrte Zeitungen	1744–1745	DiLibri
Trierisches Wochen-Blättgen	1768–1819 5 y; wide gaps	DiLibri
Triestingtaler und Priestingtaler Wochenblatt	1925–1939	ANNO
Tübinger Blätter	1901	UTUB
Tübingische gelehrte Anzeigen	1790–1792	UGOT
Türkische Post	1938; 1940–1941	ZEFYS
Überetscher Gemeindeblatt für Eppan und Kaltern	1908–1935; 1949–1974	Tessmann
Ulk	1914–1930	UHEID
Union	1872–1874	Euro
Unser Landsturm im Hennegau	1916–1917	UHEID
Unser Egerland	1897	Kram
Unsere Tribüne	1924–1926	CompMem
Unsere Zeitung	1923–1934	UpAust
Unterhaltung, Wissen und Heimat	1938	ZEFYS
Unterhaltungen	1836	UBONN
Unterhaltungs- und Anzeigerblatt für den Kreis Schleiden	1849–1866	UBONN
Unterhaltungsblatt der Neustadter Zeitung	1853–1867	GooBook

Title	Dates	Key
Unterländer Kurier	1908; 1914–1918	BNF
Vaterländische Blätter für den österreichischen Kaiserstaat	1808–1820	ANNO
Verbands-Bote	1919	Tex Cult
Vereinigte Ofner-Pester Zeitung	1814	DiFMOE
Verhandlungen des Landraths im Ober-Donau Kreis	1817–1837 (?)	GooBook
Verlustliste	1914–1919	ANNO
Verlustliste Alphabetisches Verzeichnis	1914–1919	ANNO
Verordnungs- und Anzeigeblatt der königl. Bayerischern Verkehrs-Anstalten	1867	GooBook
Verordnungs- und Anzeigeblatt für die königlich Bayerischen Posten	1845–1847	Bavarica
Verordnungs-Anzeigeblatt für den Kreis Heppenheim	1929	UDARM
Verordnungsblatt für die Beamten und Angestellten der Steuerverwalgung	1842	GooBook
Vogesenwacht	1916–1918	USTR
Vogtländischer Anzeiger und Tageblatt	1886 Aug	UHEID
Volk	1950	UJENA
Volk und Land	1919	CompMem
Volksblatt für Bergisch-Gladbach und Umgegend	1890–1906	UBONN
Volksblatt für die Kreise Bonn und Sieg	1849	UBONN
Volksblatt und Freiheits-Freund	1901–1995	GooNews
Volksbote	1920–1941	Tessmann

Title	Dates	Key
Volksmund	1906–1918	UBONN
Volksrecht	1920–1923	Tessmann
Volksstimme	1848	Euro
Volksstimme	1895–1932	FES
Volksstimme	1919 Apr-Aug	DiFMOE
Volkswacht	1912–1919	GDAN
Volkswacht für Schlesien	1891–1928; 1930–1933	FES
Volks-Zeitung	1856–1858	ZEFYS
Volks-Zeitung	1914–1943 16 y; gaps	ANNO
Volkszeitung für Sachsen-Weimar-Eisenach	1919–1920	UJENA
Volkszeitung Großherzogtum Sachsen-Weimar-Eisenach	1916–1918	UJENA
Vorarlberger Landes-Zeitung	1863–1931	Euro
Vorarlberger Volksblatt	1866–1938	ANNO
Vorarlberger Wacht	1910–1920; 1923–1938	ANNO
Vorwärts	1848–1849	DigiPress
Vossische Zeitung	1918–1934	ZEFYS
Waldbröler Kreisblatt	1855–1858; 1865–1866	UBONN
Waldbröler Kreisblatt	1862–1866	UBONN
Waldeckisches Intelligenz-Blatt	1782	Hathi

Title	Dates	Key
Waldeckisches Intelligenz-Blatt	1776–1810	UKASL
Waldenburger Wochenblatt	1883	Euro
Warhafftige und gründliche Zeitung	1620	DiLibri
Warnsdorfer Volkszeitung	1884	ANNO
Warschauer Zeitung	1859–1862	GooBook
Wartburg Herold	1896–1898	UJENA
Wasserburger Anzeiger	1871; 1873	GooBook
Wasserburger Wochenblatt	1852–1864 6 y; gaps	GooBook
Weckruf	1919 March 19	DiFMOE
Weilheimer Tagblatt für Stadt und Land	1872	GooBook
Weilheim-Werdenfelser Wochenblatt	1865–1873	GooBook
Weimarer Zeitung	1856–1863	UJENA
Weimarische Volkszeitung	1914–1916	UJENA
Weimarische wöchentliche Anzeigen	1755–1800	UJENA
Weimarische Zeitung	1832–1932	UJENA
Weimarisches Allerlei	1805	UJENA
Weimarisches Wochenblatt	1800–1832	UJENA
Wele-Neuigkeitsblatt	1881	ANNO
Weltbote	1793–1803	BNF

Title	Dates	Key
Welt-Bothe	1812 Feb 5–1818 Jan 2	NewsBank
Weser-Zeitung	1844–1845	GooBook
Weser-Zeitung	1886 Aug	UHEID
Westfälische Lehrer-Zeitung	1872–1883	UMST
Westfälisch-Schaumburgische Zeitung	1886 Aug	UHEID
Westricher Tagblatt	1855	GooBook
Westricher Zeitung	1852–1856	GooBook
Wetzlarer Kreis- und Amtsblatt	1850–1866	UBONN
Wiener Allgemeine Zeitung	1886 Aug	UHEID
Wiener Allgemeine Zeitung	1917–1919	ANNO
Wiener Bilder	1896–1939	ANNO
Wiener Caricaturen	1881–1920	ANNO
Wiener entomologische Zeitung	1883–1923	Bio
Wiener Feuerwehrzeitung	1871	ANNO
Wiener illustrirte Garten-Zeitung	1887	Bio
Wiener Montagsjournal	1911	ANNO
Wiener Morgenzeitung	1919–1927	CompMem
Wiener neueste Nachrichten	1934–1941	ANNO
Wiener Zeitung	1703–1939 223 y; gaps	ANNO

Title	Dates	Key
Wienerische Kirchenzeitung	1784–1789	Euro
Wienerisches Diarium	1703–1779	CRL
Wiesbadener Badeblatt	1867–1933	Wiesbdn
Wiesbadener Tagblatt	1905–1914	RheinMain
Wilhelmshavener Tageblatt	1886 Aug	UHEID
Windausche Zeitung	1901–1931 17 y; gaps	Latvia
Wipperfürther Kreis-Intelligenz-Blatt	1843–1867; 1870; 1883	UBONN
Wissenschaftliche Zeitschrift für jüdische Theologie	1835–1847 6 y; gaps	CompMem
Wittenbergisches Wochenblatt	1768–1785	Euro
Wochenbeilage der Darmstädter Zeitung	1906–1914; 1919–1920	UDARM
Wochenblat für den Langensalzaer Kreis	1818–1823	UJENA
Wochenblatt	1854–1873	Hathi
Wochenblatt der Frankfurter Zeitung	1914 Nov 17	Euro
Wochenblatt der Stadt Amberg	1815; 1817–1818; 1835; 1841	GooBook
Wochenblatt der Stadt Dillingen	1819–1825; 1827	Bavarica
Wochenblatt der Stadt Nördlingen	1842–1848	GooBook
Wochenblatt der Stadt Sulzbach	1852; 1865; 1872	Bavarica
Wochenblatt der Union	1866–1867	TX Hist
Wochenblatt des Bönnischen Bezirks	1808–1811	UBONN

Title	Dates	Key
Wochenblatt des Landwirtschartlichen Vereins in Bayern	1811–1840?	GooBook
Wochenblatt des Landwirtschartlichen Vereins in Bayern	1813–1818	Hathi
Wochenblatt für das Fürstenthum Oettingen-Spielberg	1843	Bavarica
Wochenblatt für das Fürstenthum Oettingen-Spielberg und die Umgebung	1844–1847	Bavarica
Wochenblatt für das Fürstenthum Sigmaringen	1809	GooBook
Wochenblatt für den Kreis Adenau und Umgegend	1855–1862	UBONN
Wochenblatt für den Kreis Malmedy	1866	BelgArch
Wochenblatt für die königlich bayerischen Landgerichtsbezirke Pfaffenhofen und Schrobenhausen	1855–1856; 1859; 1862–1862	Bavarica
Wochenblatt für die Provinz Fulda	1822–1867	UFULD
Wochen-Blatt für die Stadt und den Landgerichts-Bezirk Oettingen	1848–1853	Bavarica
Wochenblatt für Gößnitz und Umgebung	1879–1944 coming	CompMem
Wochenblatt für Land- und Hauswirthschaft, Gewerbe und Handel	1834	GooBook
Wochenblatt für Papierfabrikation	1915–1933 17 y; gaps	Hathi
Wochen-Post	1939	Euro
Wochenschrift der K.K. Gesellschaft der Ärzte	1855–1856	GooBook
Wöchentlich Oekonomisches Intelligenz-Blatt	1769–1772	UKASL
Wöchentliche Anzeigen für das Fürstenthum Ratzeburg	1856–1894	Meck Lib
Wöchentliche Ostfriesische Anzeigen und Nachrichten	1780–1781	UGOT

Title	Dates	Key
Wöchentlicher Anzeiger	1930	Ancestry
Wöchentlicher Anzeiger für die katholische Geistlichkeit	1833–1839	Bavarica
Wöchentliches Kundschaftsblatt des Herzogthums Krain	1775	Slovenia
Wöchentliches Kundschaftsblatt des Herzogthums Krain	1775–1776	Hathi
Wöchentliches Unterhaltungs-Blatt für den Kanton Dürkheim	1836	BavLib
Wöchentliches Unterhaltungs-Blatt für den Land-Commissariats-Bezirk Germersheim	1833–1834	GooBook
Wohlstand für Alle	1907–1914	A-Bib
Wormser Sport=Zeitung	1926–1929	UDARM
Wormser Tageblatt	1893–1907	UDARM
Wormser Zeitung	1838–1851; 1853–1876	UDARM
Würzburger Abendblatt	1848–1873	GooBook
Würzburger Anzeiger	1862–1868	GooBook
Würzburger Diözesanblatt	1855–2006	BavLib
Würzburger Intelligenzblatt	1805–1806; 1810–1814	GooBook
Würzburger Regierungsblatt	1806; 1809	GooBook
Würzburger Stadt- und Landbote	1873	GooBook
Würzburger Tagblatt	1857	GooBook
Ynnsbruckische Mittwochige Ordinari-Zeitung	1765	GooBook
Zabrzer Kreis-Zeitung	1907–1915	ZEFYS

Title	Dates	Key
Zabrzer Zeitung	1921–1922	ZEFYS
Zeitbilder	1918–1934	ZEFYS
Zeitblatt für die Angelegenheiten der Lutherischen Kirche	1851	GooBook
Zeitschrift des Österreichischen Ingenieur-und Architekten-Vereins	1906–1915	UCOT
Zeitschrift des Österreichischen Ingenieur-Vereins	1900–1917	UCOT
Zeitschrift für Demographie und Statistik der Juden [Alte Folge]	1905–1923 15 y; gaps	CompMem
Zeitschrift für Demographie und Statistik der Juden [Neue Folge]	1924–1927; 1930–1931	CompMem
Zeitschrift für die Geschichte der Juden in der Tschechoslowakei	1930–1934; 1938	CompMem
Zeitschrift für die Geschichte der Juden in Deutschland	1887–1937 13 y; gaps	CompMem
Zeitschrift für die Wissenschaft der Juden	1823	CompMem
Zeitung auß Wormbs	1621	DiLibri
Zeitung der 10. Armee	1915–1918	UHEID
Zeitung des Großherzogthums Frankfurt	1811–1813	GooBook
Zeitung des Landsturm-Infanterie-Bataillon Zittau	1915	BNF
Zeitung des Vereins deutscher Eisenbahn-Verwaltungen	1900	GooBook
Zeitung für den deutschen Adel	1840; 1842–1844	GooBook
Zeitung für Feuerlöschwesen	1868–1873	GooBook
Zeitung für Landwirtschaft	1877–1904	ANNO
Zeitungszeugen	1933–1945	Zzgn

Title	Dates	Key
Zentral- und Bezirks Amtsblatt für Elsaß-Lothringen	1883–1918	BavLib
Zentral- und Bezirks Amtsblatt für Elsaß-Lothringen	1884–1904	GooBook
Zentral- und Bezirks Amtsblatt für Elsaß-Lothringen	1914–1918	BNF
Zion	1929–1938	CompMem
Znaimer Tagblatt	1898–1919; 1939–1943	ANNO
Znaimer Wochenblatt	1858–1919	ANNO
Zniner Zeitung	1891–1920 20 y; gaps	Euro
Zülpicher Anzeiger	1867–1868	UBONN
Zürcherisches Wochenblatt	1803–1842	GooBook
Zweibrücker Tagblatt	1869–1870	GooBook
Zweibrücker Zeitung	1832–1833; 1871–1872	GooBook
Zweybrückische Zeitung	1786	GooBook
Zweybrückisches Wochenblatt (and variants)	1767–1870 42 y; major gaps	GooBook
Zwischen Maas und Mosel	1918 Mar	USTR

CPSIA information can be obtained at www.ICGtesting.com
Printed in the USA
LVOW04s0924181015

458736LV00021B/766/P

9 780806 320052